# COOKING AT HOME WITH
# Bridget & Julia

The TV Hosts of *America's Test Kitchen*
Share Their Favorite Recipes for Feeding Family and Friends

BRIDGET LANCASTER
JULIA COLLIN DAVISON
*and the Editors at*
AMERICA'S TEST KITCHEN

Copyright © 2017

by Bridget Lancaster, Julia Collin Davison,
and the Editors at America's Test Kitchen

Library of Congress Cataloging-in-Publication Data

Names: Lancaster, Bridget, author. | Davison, Julia Collin, author. |
  America's Test Kitchen (Firm)

Title: Cooking at home with Bridget & Julia : the tv hosts of America's
  test kitchen share their favorite recipes for feeding family and friends /
  Bridget Lancaster, Julia Collin Davison, and the editors at America's
  Test Kitchen.

Other titles: America's test kitchen (Television program)

Description: Boston, MA : America's Test Kitchen, [2017] | Includes
  bibliographical references and index.

Identifiers: LCCN 2017018306 | ISBN 9781945256165 (alk. paper)

Subjects: LCSH: Cooking. | LCGFT: Cookbooks.

Classification: LCC TX714 .L3396 2017 | DDC 641.5--dc23

LC record available at https://lccn.loc.gov/2017018306

AMERICA'S TEST KITCHEN

AMERICA'S TEST KITCHEN

21 Drydock Avenue, Suite 210E, Boston, MA 02210

Manufactured in the United States of America

10 9 8 7 6 5 4 3 2 1

Distributed by Penguin Random House Publisher Services
Tel: 800.733.3000

CHIEF CREATIVE OFFICER  Jack Bishop

EDITORIAL DIRECTOR, BOOKS  Elizabeth Carduff

SENIOR MANAGING EDITOR  Debra Hudak

ASSOCIATE EDITOR  Melissa Drumm

EDITORIAL ASSISTANT  Alyssa Langer

DESIGN DIRECTOR  Carole Goodman

DEPUTY ART DIRECTORS  Allison Boales and Jen Kanavos Hoffman

PHOTOGRAPHY DIRECTOR  Julie Bozzo Cote

PHOTOGRAPHY PRODUCER  Mary Ball

SENIOR STAFF PHOTOGRAPHER  Daniel J. van Ackere

STAFF PHOTOGRAPHERS  Steve Klise and Kevin White

ADDITIONAL PHOTOGRAPHY  Keller + Keller and Carl Tremblay

FOOD STYLING  Catrine Kelty, Kendra McKnight, Marie Piraino,
Elle Simone Scott, and Sally Staub

PHOTO SHOOT KITCHEN TEAM

    MANAGER  Timothy McQuinn

    SENIOR EDITOR  Chris O'Connor

    LEAD COOK  Daniel Cellucci

    ASSISTANT TEST COOKS  Mady Nichas and Jessica Rudolph

LOCATION PHOTOGRAPHY TEAM

    PHOTOGRAPHER  Carl Tremblay

    FOOD AND PROP STYLING  Catrine Kelty and Sally Staub

    WARDROBE  Honah Lee Milne

    HAIR  Jennifer Tawa, Patrice Vinci Salon, and Grace Callan

    MAKEUP  Claudia Moriel

PRODUCTION DIRECTOR  Guy Rochford

SENIOR PRODUCTION MANAGER  Jessica Lindheimer Quirk

PRODUCTION MANAGER  Christine Walsh

IMAGING MANAGER  Lauren Robbins

PRODUCTION AND IMAGING SPECIALISTS  Heather Dube, Dennis Noble,
and Jessica Voas

COPY EDITOR  Cheryl Redmond

PROOFREADER  Jane Tunks Demel

INDEXER  Elizabeth Parson

# contents

*Bridget and Julia filming season 17 of the TV show.*

# a note from bridget and julia

We've kind of grown up here at America's Test Kitchen. We started cooking and developing recipes during the test kitchen's early days, when we were just starting our careers. Now, nearly 20 years later, we are the hosts of the company's two hugely popular TV shows. Along the way, we've developed a lot of recipes and cooked hundreds more on set. People always ask us which recipes are our favorites and why. Our new special collection, *Cooking at Home with Bridget and Julia*, answers that very question. It features 150 recipes (75 from each of us) from the test kitchen's archives that we cook at home time and time again. The process of choosing and writing about these recipes has led us on an interesting journey because the recipes we love are connected to how and where we were raised, where we have traveled, and what we like to cook for our husbands and children. So you'll learn more about us by reading this book. Personal facts abound in the narratives accompanying each recipe, like how Bridget became addicted to Indian food on a trip to Scotland to meet her future husband's parents, which is why she picked Chicken Tikka Masala. A family trip to Tuscany in her teens showed Julia the power of a simple fresh tomato sauce, which is why she chose Skillet Campanelle with Fresh Tomato Sauce, a recipe that brings her back to that time and place whenever she makes it.

Cooking for us is about feeding family and friends. And since we like to pull out all the stops on occasion, you'll find a chapter devoted to holiday celebrations as well as one covering casual entertaining. We tell you which appetizers make the cut for our parties (Bacon and Chive Deviled Eggs and Stuffed Mushrooms with Boursin and Prosciutto); which main courses never disappoint (Pasta with Classic Bolognese and Slow-Roasted Pork Shoulder with Peach Sauce); which stunning desserts are a must on our holiday table (Coconut Layer Cake and Goat Cheese and Lemon Cheesecake with Hazelnut Crust); and much, much more. In addition, as working mothers, we have to put dinner on the table every night so we appreciate rock-solid, easy-to-execute recipes: Spaghetti with Turkey-Pesto Meatballs is on heavy rotation at Julia's house while Thai Pork Lettuce Wraps are a favorite of Bridget's two sons. You'll find these recipes and more among the home-style dinners, while the weekend breakfast chapter tells you just what we like to eat on a lazy Sunday morning.

We hope you enjoy both this collection and getting to know us better. We love to cook and think you'll share our enthusiasm for the work we do here at America's Test Kitchen.

*Bridget Lancaster and Julia Collin Davison*

# meet bridget

I know that I'm blessed. I have a loving husband, two beautiful sons, and a big, handsome hunk of a dog. We live in a close-knit community where folks still visit their neighbors and parents look out for the kids. Think Mayberry-by-the-Sea.

Before I started at ATK I worked two jobs—as a restaurant pastry chef and as a stock worker for Williams-Sonoma, where I assisted with celebrity chef visits. Once a winter ice storm threatened to cancel a visit from Julia Child, so a coworker and I set out to retrieve her.

Julia's driveway was a sheet of ice, and we literally held her up as we slid to the car. I felt two simultaneous emotions: humbled to walk with this national treasure, and terrified that I would be known as the person who let Julia Child fall. We arrived unscathed, and Julia's wicked sense of humor solidified her as one of my idols.

I grew up in a middle-class West Virginia neighborhood. It was my mother who taught me not only to cook, but to be grateful to have food to eat at all. She delivered food and clothing from our church to communities in crisis and brought me along so that I could see what real hunger looked like and remember that it was never that far away.

That experience still impacts my view of the food world. No matter the exotic ingredients or involved cooking technique, it's food that allows us to live, and even thrive.

So to have an interesting, challenging, ever-changing, and, yes, fun, job, where I get to talk food with some of the most fascinating people that a person could meet—well, I'd say that I am blessed, indeed.

# meet julia

I come from a long line of great cooks (and good eaters). The best cook of them all is my mother, Winifred, who has always been a bit ahead of her time, growing organic vegetables, grinding meat for hamburgers, and steering clear of processed foods. My love of cooking really came from hanging out with her in the kitchen as I grew up in Rochester, New York.

I didn't immediately see that my love of cooking could be the foundation of my career, but it eventually dawned on me. After graduating from college, where I studied philosophy, psychology, and music (also known as "splashing around in the fountain of knowledge" by my father), nothing was catching fire in terms of a direction. So I decided to go to culinary school at the Culinary Institute of America in Hyde Park, New York—that appealed to my practical side and to the fact that I liked to use my hands to do something creative, namely cooking.

My job at America's Test Kitchen followed shortly thereafter, thanks again (in part) to my mother. As a long time fan of *Cook's Illustrated*, she urged me to apply for a Test Cook position in the late 90s. Thank goodness I took her advice! Not only do I love developing recipes, but as it turns out, I also love teaching. Before long, I was leading the cookbook team in the test kitchen, cooking on both of our TV shows, and developing my own strong opinions about food.

Whenever I taste a recipe, I ask myself how it will work for folks at home. Will it solve a common cooking problem, help get dinner on the table, or offer some solid advice on a tricky topic? For this collection, I've chosen recipes that taught me something; I've grown so much as a cook since I began working here nearly two decades ago. These recipes regularly grace my table at home, and I hope you will enjoy them as much as I do.

# listing of recipes

# home-style dinners

# casual entertaining

# holiday celebrations

# weekend breakfasts

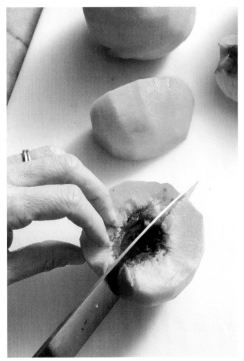

# dutch baby

serves 4

2 tablespoons vegetable oil

1 cup (5 ounces) all-purpose flour

¼ cup (1 ounce) cornstarch

2 teaspoons grated lemon zest plus 2 tablespoons juice

1 teaspoon salt

3 large eggs

1¼ cups skim milk

1 tablespoon unsalted butter, melted and cooled

1 teaspoon vanilla extract

3 tablespoons confectioners' sugar

" My grandfather served in the army during World War II (42nd Rainbow Division), and after the war he and his family were stationed in Gelnhausen, Germany. When he returned to the States, he brought with him a love of Bavarian food, including *pfannkuchen* (literally 'pan cake') also known as a Dutch baby. This isn't your usual American pancake; it's a skillet-size, gossamer-thin, supercrisp confection that you're apparently supposed to share with other folks at the table. All I know is that once that Dutch baby gets a squeeze of lemon and a huge shower of confectioners' sugar… IT'S ALL MINE! "

*bridget*

1  Adjust oven rack to middle position and heat oven to 450 degrees. Brush bottom and sides of 12-inch skillet with oil. Heat skillet in oven until oil is shimmering, about 10 minutes.

2  Meanwhile, combine flour, cornstarch, lemon zest, and salt in large bowl. Whisk eggs in second bowl until frothy and light, about 1 minute. Whisk milk, melted butter, and vanilla into eggs until incorporated. Whisk one-third of milk mixture into flour mixture until no lumps remain, then slowly whisk in remaining milk mixture until smooth.

3  Carefully pour batter into skillet and bake until edges are deep golden brown and crisp, about 20 minutes. Transfer skillet to wire rack, sprinkle pancake with lemon juice and confectioners' sugar, and cut into wedges. Serve.

*Cooking at Home with Bridget and Julia*

# buttermilk pancakes

serves 4 to 6

2 cups (10 ounces) all-purpose flour

2 tablespoons sugar

2 teaspoons baking powder

½ teaspoon baking soda

½ teaspoon salt

2 cups buttermilk

3 tablespoons unsalted butter, melted and cooled

1 large egg

1–2 teaspoons vegetable oil

"

My daughter, Marta, and I make these on the weekends a few times a month. She sits right on top of the counter and does all the measuring and whisking. We usually make quite a mess, but it's good fun and the pancakes taste terrific. I prefer this recipe over the other ATK pancake recipes because it's so darn easy and it doesn't require any serious kitchen equipment. Everything just gets mixed together in big bowls, which is the right level of difficulty for Marta and me on a Saturday morning. I rarely have fresh buttermilk on hand so I use powdered buttermilk instead; it works like a charm. "

*julia*

1  Adjust oven rack to middle position and heat oven to 200 degrees. Spray wire rack with vegetable oil spray, set in rimmed baking sheet, and place in oven.

2  Whisk flour, sugar, baking powder, baking soda, and salt together in large bowl. Whisk buttermilk, melted butter, and egg together in large measuring cup. Make well in center of dry ingredients, add wet ingredients to well, and gently stir until just combined. Do not overmix; batter should be lumpy with few streaks of flour.

3  Heat 1 teaspoon oil in 12-inch nonstick skillet over medium heat until shimmering. Using paper towels, carefully wipe out oil, leaving thin film of oil on bottom and sides of pan. Using ¼-cup dry measure, portion batter into pan in 3 places. Cook until edges are set, first side is golden, and bubbles on surface are just beginning to break, 2 to 3 minutes.

4  Flip pancakes and continue to cook until second side is golden, 1 to 2 minutes. Serve immediately or transfer to wire rack in oven. Repeat with remaining batter, using remaining oil as necessary.

# yeasted waffles

serves 4

1¾ cups milk

8 tablespoons unsalted butter, cut into 8 pieces

2 cups (10 ounces) all-purpose flour

1 tablespoon sugar

1½ teaspoons instant or rapid-rise yeast

1 teaspoon salt

2 large eggs

1 teaspoon vanilla extract

"

I fondly remember my Uncle Alan making waffles for us at our summer cabin in the Berkshires. He only prepared this big breakfast once a year and we all really looked forward to it. I loved how the sweet scent of waffles was in the air when we woke up, and there were tall stacks of waffles waiting for us in the kitchen. There's no electricity at the cabin, so he used an old waffle maker that sat right on the stovetop. He always made yeasted waffles, much like this recipe. The batter sits overnight and develops an incredible flavor that you just can't get with a quick waffle batter, and the waffle edges turn out supercrisp and light. I've found that these waffles also freeze well, and can be reheated quickly in a toaster. "

*julia*

1  Heat milk and butter in small saucepan over medium-low heat until butter is melted, 3 to 5 minutes. Let mixture cool until warm to touch.

2  Whisk flour, sugar, yeast, and salt together in large bowl. In small bowl, whisk eggs and vanilla together. Gradually whisk warm milk mixture into flour mixture until smooth, then whisk in egg mixture. Scrape down bowl with rubber spatula, cover tightly with plastic wrap, and refrigerate for at least 12 hours or up to 1 day.

3  Adjust oven rack to middle position and heat oven to 200 degrees. Set wire rack in rimmed baking sheet and place in oven. Heat waffle iron according to manufacturer's instructions. Remove batter from refrigerator when waffle iron is hot (batter will be foamy and doubled in size). Whisk batter to recombine (batter will deflate).

4  Cook waffles according to manufacturer's instructions (use about ½ cup batter for 7-inch round iron and about 1 cup batter for 9-inch square iron). Serve immediately or transfer to wire rack in oven to keep warm while cooking remaining waffles.

# apple fritters

serves 10

## fritters

2 Granny Smith apples, peeled, cored, halved, and cut into ¼-inch pieces

2 cups (10 ounces) all-purpose flour

⅓ cup (2⅓ ounces) granulated sugar

1 tablespoon baking powder

1 teaspoon salt

1 teaspoon ground cinnamon

¼ teaspoon ground nutmeg

¾ cup apple cider

2 large eggs, lightly beaten

2 tablespoons unsalted butter, melted and cooled

3 cups vegetable oil

## glaze

2 cups (8 ounces) confectioners' sugar

¼ cup apple cider

½ teaspoon ground cinnamon

¼ teaspoon ground nutmeg

1 **For the fritters** Spread apples in single layer on paper towel–lined rimmed baking sheet and pat dry thoroughly with more paper towels. Whisk flour, sugar, baking powder, salt, cinnamon, and nutmeg together in large bowl. In separate bowl, whisk cider, eggs, and melted butter together. Add apples to flour mixture to coat, then stir in cider mixture until incorporated.

2 Heat oil in large Dutch oven over medium-high heat to 350 degrees. Set wire rack in clean rimmed baking sheet. Using ⅓-cup dry measure, transfer 5 heaping portions of batter to oil. Press batter lightly with back of spoon to flatten. Fry, adjusting burner as necessary to maintain oil temperature between 325 and 350 degrees, until deep golden brown, 2 to 3 minutes per side.

3 Transfer fritters to prepared wire rack. Return oil to 350 degrees and repeat with remaining batter.

4 **For the glaze** Whisk all ingredients in bowl until smooth. Top each fritter with 1 heaping tablespoon glaze. Let glaze set for 10 minutes before serving.

# muffin tin doughnuts

makes 12 doughnuts

## doughnuts

2¾ cups (13¾ ounces) all-purpose flour

1 cup (7 ounces) sugar

¼ cup (1 ounce) cornstarch

1 tablespoon baking powder

1 teaspoon salt

½ teaspoon ground nutmeg

1 cup buttermilk

8 tablespoons unsalted butter, melted

2 large eggs plus 1 large yolk

## coating

1 cup sugar

2 teaspoons ground cinnamon

8 tablespoons unsalted butter, melted

1  **For the doughnuts**  Adjust oven rack to middle position and heat oven to 400 degrees. Grease 12-cup muffin tin. Whisk flour, sugar, cornstarch, baking powder, salt, and nutmeg together in large bowl. In separate bowl, whisk buttermilk, melted butter, and eggs and yolk together. Add buttermilk mixture to flour mixture and stir with rubber spatula until just combined.

2  Divide batter evenly among muffin cups. Bake until lightly browned and toothpick inserted in center comes out clean, 19 to 22 minutes, rotating muffin tin halfway through baking. Let doughnuts cool in muffin tin for 5 minutes.

3  **For the coating**  Whisk sugar and cinnamon together in bowl. Remove doughnuts from muffin tin. Working with 1 doughnut at a time, brush completely with melted butter, then roll in cinnamon sugar, pressing lightly to adhere. Transfer to wire rack and let cool for 15 minutes. Serve.

> What's up with muffins? I mean, they bake like a cupcake, and they look like a cupcake, but when you get close enough, you realize that the 'cupcake' has no frosting on top and it is indeed a muffin!! Even worse is a 'healthy' muffin. So I was skeptical about a muffin that was trying to mimic a doughnut (we've already established my doughnut addiction). But these really deliver. And you know why? Butter. Yep, lots of butter brushed over the exteriors of the doughnuts followed by a romp in some cinnamon sugar gives these a crunchy, sugary crust–almost like a real doughnut. "

*bridget*

# beignets

makes 24 beignets

1 cup warm water (110 degrees)

3 tablespoons granulated sugar

1 tablespoon instant or
rapid-rise yeast

3 cups (15 ounces) all-purpose flour

¾ teaspoon salt

2 large eggs

2 tablespoons plus 2 quarts
vegetable oil

Confectioners' sugar

66

We started making these at our house when Marta was younger and her favorite movie was *The Princess and the Frog*. The movie is set in New Orleans and the princess is also a wonderful cook who is known for her beignets. The princess and her friend agree that the best way to win a man is 'through his stomach,' so she makes platters of 'man-catching beignets' to help her friend win the heart of the visiting prince. It's a good movie and I always refer to beignets as 'man-catchers.' I like this version of the recipe because it's simple to put together and the dough is easy to work with. I like to serve them with powdered sugar, as the recipe suggests, but Marta likes to drizzle hers with honey. 99

*julia*

1  Combine warm water, 1 tablespoon granulated sugar, and yeast in large bowl and let sit until foamy, about 5 minutes. In separate bowl, combine flour, salt, and remaining 2 tablespoons granulated sugar. Whisk eggs and 2 tablespoons oil into yeast mixture. Add flour mixture and stir vigorously with rubber spatula until dough comes together. Cover tightly with plastic wrap and refrigerate until dough has nearly doubled in size, about 1 hour.

2  Set wire rack in rimmed baking sheet. Line second sheet with parchment paper and dust heavily with flour. Transfer dough to generously floured counter and cut in half. Working with 1 piece of dough at a time, pat into rough rectangle with your floured hands, flipping to coat with flour. Roll dough into ¼-inch-thick rectangle roughly 12 by 9 inches in size. Using pizza wheel, cut dough into twelve 3-inch squares and transfer to floured sheet.

3  Add remaining 2 quarts oil to large Dutch oven until it measures about 1½ inches deep and heat over medium-high heat to 350 degrees. Working in batches of six, fry beignets until golden brown, about 3 minutes, flipping halfway through frying; transfer to prepared wire rack. Dust with confectioners' sugar and serve warm.

# potato, swiss chard, and lamb hash with poached eggs

serves 4

"

Ian and I love eating hash with a fried egg on top for breakfast, lunch, or dinner. Over the years, we've played with the traditional corned beef hash by swapping in other kinds of ingredients (sweet potatoes, cauliflower, kale, chorizo, ham, tempeh) for the potatoes and corned beef. This lamb hash with potatoes and chard is a great example of an easy dinnertime hash, and I love how quickly it comes together. It's important to cook the ingredients separately before combining them or else you wind up with mush instead of hash. We serve this with lots of hot sauce. "

*julia*

1½ pounds russet potatoes, peeled and cut into ½-inch pieces

2 tablespoons extra-virgin olive oil

Salt and pepper

1½ pounds Swiss chard, stems sliced ¼ inch thick, leaves sliced into ½-inch-wide strips

8 ounces ground lamb

1 onion, chopped fine

3 garlic cloves, minced

2 teaspoons paprika

1 teaspoon ground cumin

1 teaspoon ground coriander

¼ teaspoon cayenne pepper

4 large eggs

1 tablespoon minced fresh chives

1  Toss potatoes with 1 tablespoon oil, ½ teaspoon salt, and ¼ teaspoon pepper in bowl. Cover and microwave until potatoes are translucent around edges, 7 to 9 minutes, stirring halfway through microwaving; drain well.

2  Heat remaining 1 tablespoon oil in 12-inch nonstick skillet over medium-high heat until shimmering. Add chard stems and ¼ teaspoon salt and cook until softened and lightly browned, 5 to 7 minutes. Stir in chard leaves, a handful at a time, and cook until mostly wilted, about 4 minutes; transfer to bowl with potatoes.

3  Cook lamb in now-empty skillet over medium-high heat, breaking up meat with wooden spoon, until beginning to brown, about 5 minutes. Stir in onion and cook until softened and lightly browned, 5 to 7 minutes. Stir in garlic, paprika, cumin, coriander, and cayenne and cook until fragrant, about 30 seconds.

4  Stir in chard-potato mixture. Using back of spatula, gently pack chard-potato mixture into skillet and cook, without stirring, for 2 minutes. Flip hash, 1 portion at a time, and lightly repack into skillet. Repeat flipping process every few minutes until potatoes are well browned, 6 to 8 minutes.

5  Off heat, make 4 shallow indentations (about 2 inches wide) in hash using back of spoon, pushing hash up into center and around edges of skillet (bottom of skillet should be exposed in each divot). Crack 1 egg into each indentation and season with salt and pepper. Cover and cook over medium-low heat until whites are just set and yolks are still runny, 4 to 5 minutes. Sprinkle with chives and serve immediately.

# huevos rancheros

serves 2 to 4

After graduating from culinary school, I spent some time working in San Francisco and Napa and fell in love with Mexican food. When I lived there, it felt like there was great Mexican food on nearly every corner. Here in Boston, however, I quickly realized that if I wanted to eat good Mexican food, I had to make it myself. This huevos rancheros recipe is one of my favorites because the sauce has a clean, fresh tomato flavor and the method for cooking the eggs in the oven is very clever. This recipe also uses the oven to toast the tortillas, which is easy and works well, but I prefer to fry the tortillas in oil. I serve this with diced avocado, sliced scallions, and hot sauce. "

*julia*

## salsa

3 jalapeño chiles, stemmed, halved, and seeded

1½ pounds plum tomatoes, cored and halved

½ onion, cut into ½-inch wedges through root end

2 tablespoons vegetable oil

1 tablespoon tomato paste

2 garlic cloves, peeled

Salt and pepper

½ teaspoon ground cumin

⅛ teaspoon cayenne pepper

3 tablespoons minced fresh cilantro

1-2 tablespoons lime juice, plus lime wedges for serving

## tortillas and eggs

4 (6-inch) corn tortillas

1 tablespoon vegetable oil

Salt and pepper

4 large eggs

**1 For the salsa** Adjust oven rack to middle position and heat oven to 375 degrees. Mince 1 jalapeño; set aside. Toss remaining 2 jalapeños, tomatoes, onion, oil, tomato paste, garlic, 1 teaspoon salt, cumin, and cayenne together in bowl. Arrange vegetables cut side down on rimmed baking sheet. Roast until tomatoes are tender and skins begin to shrivel and brown, 35 to 45 minutes.

**2** Let roasted vegetables cool on sheet for 10 minutes. Process onion, garlic, and jalapeños in food processor until almost completely broken down, about 10 seconds. Add tomatoes and process until salsa is slightly chunky, about 10 seconds. Stir in minced jalapeño and 2 tablespoons cilantro. Season with salt, pepper, and lime juice to taste. (Salsa can be refrigerated for up to 1 day.)

**3 For the tortillas and eggs** Increase oven temperature to 450 degrees. Brush both sides of each tortilla lightly with oil, sprinkle with salt, and place on clean baking sheet. Bake until tops just begin to color, 5 to 7 minutes. Flip tortillas and continue to bake until golden, 2 to 3 minutes. Remove tortillas from oven and cover sheet with aluminum foil to keep tortillas warm.

**4** Meanwhile, bring salsa to gentle simmer in 12-inch nonstick skillet over medium heat. Off heat, make 4 shallow indentations (about 2 inches wide) in salsa using back of spoon. Crack 1 egg into each indentation and season with salt and pepper. Cover and cook over medium-low heat until eggs are cooked through, 4 to 5 minutes for runny yolks or 6 to 7 minutes for set yolks.

**5** Place tortillas on individual serving plates and gently top with cooked eggs. Spoon salsa around eggs to cover tortillas. Sprinkle with remaining 1 tablespoon cilantro. Serve with lime wedges.

# perfect french omelet

serves 2

2 tablespoons unsalted butter, cut into 2 pieces

½ teaspoon vegetable oil

6 large eggs, chilled

Salt and pepper

2 tablespoons shredded Gruyère cheese

4 teaspoons minced fresh chives

1  Adjust oven rack to middle position and heat oven to 200 degrees. Place 2 heatproof plates on rack.

2  Cut 1 tablespoon butter in half. Cut remaining 1 tablespoon butter into small pieces, transfer to small bowl, and place in freezer while preparing eggs and skillet, at least 10 minutes.

3  Meanwhile, heat oil in 8-inch nonstick skillet over low heat for 10 minutes. Crack 2 eggs into medium bowl and separate third egg; add egg yolk to bowl and discard white. Add ⅛ teaspoon salt and pinch pepper. Break egg yolks with fork, then use fork to beat eggs at moderate pace, about 80 strokes, until yolks and whites are well combined. Stir in half of frozen butter cubes.

4  When skillet is fully heated, use paper towels to wipe out oil, leaving thin film on bottom and sides of skillet. Melt ½ tablespoon reserved butter in skillet, swirling butter to coat. Add egg mixture and increase heat to medium-high. Use 2 chopsticks or wooden skewers to scramble eggs, using quick circular motion to move around skillet, scraping cooked egg from side of skillet as you go, until eggs are almost cooked but still slightly runny, 45 to 90 seconds. Turn off heat (remove skillet from heat if using electric burner) and smooth eggs into even layer using heat-resistant rubber spatula. Sprinkle omelet with 1 tablespoon Gruyère and 2 teaspoons chives. Cover skillet with tight-fitting lid and let sit for 1 minute for runnier omelet or 2 minutes for firmer omelet.

5  Heat skillet over low heat for 20 seconds, uncover, and, using rubber spatula, loosen edges of omelet from skillet. Place folded paper towel onto warmed plate and slide omelet out of skillet onto paper towel so that omelet lies flat on plate and hangs about 1 inch off paper towel. Using paper towel, roll omelet into neat cylinder and set aside. Return skillet to low heat and heat for 2 minutes before repeating instructions for second omelet, starting with step 3. Serve.

*Cooking at Home with Bridget and Julia*

# eggs in a hole

makes 6 toasts

6 slices hearty white sandwich bread

5 tablespoons unsalted butter, softened

6 large eggs

Salt and pepper

I'd never heard of this recipe before working at ATK, but I took to it like a duck to water. It's just a great way to make a fried egg in the morning alongside a piece of buttery toast. Using a skillet to make one or two eggs in a hole is fine, but this smart recipe uses the oven so that you can feed a crowd. Using two baking sheets is key here so that the eggs cook through evenly and gently. If you don't have a biscuit cutter, cut the toast holes with a drinking glass. **"**

*julia*

1  Adjust oven racks to top and lowest positions, place rimmed baking sheet on lower rack, and heat oven to 500 degrees. Spread 1 side of bread slices evenly with 2½ tablespoons butter. Using 2½-inch biscuit cutter, cut out and remove circle from center of each piece of buttered bread.

2  Remove hot sheet from oven, add remaining 2½ tablespoons butter, and let melt, tilting sheet to cover pan evenly. Place bread circles down center of sheet and bread slices on either side of circles, buttered side up. Return sheet to lower oven rack and bake until bread is golden, 3 to 5 minutes, flipping bread and rotating sheet halfway through baking.

3  Remove sheet from oven and set inside second (room-temperature) rimmed baking sheet. Crack 1 egg into each bread hole. Season with salt and pepper. Bake on upper rack until whites are barely set, 4 to 6 minutes, rotating sheet halfway through baking.

4  Transfer sheets to wire rack and let eggs sit until whites are completely set, about 2 minutes. Serve.

# soft-cooked eggs

makes 4 eggs

4 large eggs
Salt and pepper

1 Bring ½ inch water to boil in medium saucepan over medium-high heat. Using tongs, gently place eggs in boiling water (eggs will not be submerged). Cover saucepan and cook eggs for 6½ minutes.

2 Remove cover, transfer saucepan to sink, and place under cold running water for 30 seconds. Remove eggs from pan and serve, seasoning with salt and pepper to taste.

"

Many years ago, my husband, Stephen, was the chef at the British Embassy in Washington, D.C. He was privileged to cook for many heads of state, including the late British Prime Minister Margaret Thatcher. Politics aside, Stephen was responsible for Mrs. Thatcher's daily breakfast, which often consisted of soft-cooked eggs, 'soldiers' (toast that is cut into strips for easy dunking into the egg yolks), and black coffee. These days, he makes that very same breakfast for me, which makes me the most powerful woman in the world, right? "

*bridget*

# spanish tortilla with roasted red peppers and peas

serves 4 to 6

6 tablespoons plus 1 teaspoon extra-virgin olive oil

1½ pounds Yukon Gold potatoes, peeled, quartered, and cut into ⅛-inch-thick slices

1 small onion, halved and sliced thin

Salt and pepper

8 large eggs

½ cup jarred roasted red peppers, rinsed, patted dry, and cut into ½-inch pieces

½ cup frozen peas, thawed

> This Spanish tortilla is my go-to for an easy brunch or dinner. The tortillas I've made in the past were always pretty greasy because the traditional recipes I found used lots of olive oil (up to several cups). This recipe, however, only uses about 6 tablespoons, which I appreciate. Also, I've made them with different types of potatoes over the years and agree that Yukon Golds are the best choice because they have a buttery flavor and silky texture. Traditional recipes for tortilla often omit the roasted red peppers and peas, but I think they are nice additions here. The tortilla tastes terrific both warm and at room temperature, and adding a simple green salad turns it into dinner. Be sure to serve it with the Garlic Mayonnaise. 99
>
> *julia*

1  Toss ¼ cup oil, potatoes, onion, ½ teaspoon salt, and ¼ teaspoon pepper together in bowl. Heat 2 tablespoons oil in 10-inch nonstick skillet over medium-high heat until shimmering. Add potato mixture to pan and reduce heat to medium-low. Cover and cook, stirring every 5 minutes, until potatoes are tender, about 25 minutes.

2  Whisk eggs and ½ teaspoon salt together in now-empty bowl, then gently fold in cooked potato mixture, red peppers, and peas. Make sure to scrape all of potato mixture out of skillet.

3  Heat remaining 1 teaspoon oil in now-empty skillet over medium-high heat until just smoking. Add egg mixture and cook, shaking pan and folding mixture constantly for 15 seconds. Smooth top of egg mixture, reduce heat to medium, cover, and cook, gently shaking pan every 30 seconds, until bottom is golden brown and top is lightly set, about 2 minutes.

4  Off heat, run heatproof rubber spatula around edge of pan and shake pan gently to loosen tortilla; it should slide around freely in pan. Slide tortilla onto large plate, then invert onto second large plate and slide back into skillet browned side up. Tuck edges of tortilla into skillet with rubber spatula. Continue to cook over medium heat, gently shaking pan every 30 seconds, until second side is golden brown, about 2 minutes. Slide tortilla onto cutting board and let cool slightly. Serve warm or at room temperature.

## garlic mayonnaise

makes about 1¼ cups

2 large egg yolks

2 teaspoons Dijon mustard

2 teaspoons lemon juice

1 garlic clove, minced

¾ cup vegetable oil

1 tablespoon water

¼ cup extra-virgin olive oil

½ teaspoon salt

¼ teaspoon pepper

Process egg yolks, mustard, lemon juice, and garlic in food processor until combined, about 10 seconds. With processor running, slowly drizzle in vegetable oil, about 1 minute. Transfer mixture to medium bowl and whisk in water. Whisking constantly, slowly drizzle in olive oil, about 30 seconds. Whisk in salt and pepper. (Mayonnaise can be refrigerated for up to 4 days.)

# corned beef hash

serves 4

2 pounds russet potatoes, peeled and cut into ½-inch dice

Salt and pepper

4 slices bacon, chopped fine

1 onion, chopped fine

2 garlic cloves, minced

½ teaspoon minced fresh thyme

1 pound corned beef, cut into ¼-inch dice

½ cup heavy cream

¼ teaspoon hot sauce

4 large eggs

1  Bring potatoes, 5 cups water, and ½ teaspoon salt to boil in medium saucepan over medium-high heat. Once boiling, cook potatoes for 4 minutes, then drain and set potatoes aside.

2  Cook bacon in 12-inch non-stick skillet over medium-high heat for 2 minutes. Add onion and cook until browned, about 8 minutes. Add garlic and thyme and cook for 30 seconds. Stir in corned beef. Mix in potatoes and lightly pack mixture with spatula. Reduce heat to medium and pour heavy cream and hot sauce evenly over hash. Cook undis-turbed for 4 minutes, then, with spatula, invert hash, 1 portion at a time, and fold browned bits back into hash. Lightly pack hash into pan. Repeat process every minute or two until potatoes are cooked, about 8 minutes longer.

3  Make 4 indentations equally spaced on surface of hash. Crack 1 egg into each indentation and sprinkle eggs with salt and pepper. Reduce heat to medium-low, cover pan, and cook until eggs are just set, about 6 minutes. Cut into 4 wedges, making sure each wedge contains 1 egg, and serve.

# eggs florentine

serves 4

> Eggs Florentine is an old-school hotel brunch dish, and traditional recipes layer creamed spinach, a poached egg, and hollandaise on top of an English muffin, much like eggs Benedict. This updated recipe, however, is a modern take on the old classic and is my kind of food. Instead of creamed spinach, the toasted English muffin is topped with lemony goat cheese before being topped with sautéed baby spinach and a poached egg. I like to use an egg poaching machine (don't judge; they're awesome) rather than the traditional skillet poaching method because it's easier. Also, I'm fussy about English muffins and hate how many brands have an awful, chemical aftertaste. My favorite English muffins are also the test kitchen's winning brand, Bays; they are refrigerated and are usually found on the shelf next to the eggs at the grocery store. You will need a 12-inch nonstick skillet with a tight-fitting lid for this recipe. The vinegar in the egg poaching water adds more than just flavor—it lowers the pH in the water, ensuring that the egg whites stay intact during cooking. 

*julia*

2 ounces goat cheese, crumbled (½ cup)

½ teaspoon lemon juice

Salt and pepper

2 English muffins, split, toasted, and still warm

1 tomato, cored, seeded, and sliced thin (about 8 slices)

2 teaspoons olive oil

1 shallot, minced

1 garlic clove, minced

4 ounces (4 cups) baby spinach

2 tablespoons distilled white vinegar

4 large eggs

**1** Adjust oven rack to middle position and heat oven to 300 degrees. Combine goat cheese, lemon juice, and ⅛ teaspoon pepper in bowl until smooth. Spread goat cheese mixture evenly over English muffins, top with tomato, and arrange on baking sheet; keep warm in oven.

**2** Heat oil in 12-inch nonstick skillet over medium heat until shimmering. Add shallot and cook until softened, about 2 minutes. Stir in garlic and cook until fragrant, about 30 seconds. Stir in spinach and ⅛ teaspoon salt and cook until wilted, about 1 minute. Using tongs, squeeze out any excess moisture from spinach and divide evenly among English muffins.

**3** Wipe skillet clean with paper towels and fill it nearly to rim with water. Add vinegar and 1 teaspoon salt and bring to boil over high heat. Meanwhile, crack eggs into 2 teacups (2 eggs per cup). Reduce water to simmer. Gently tip cups so eggs slide into skillet simultaneously. Remove skillet from heat, cover, and let eggs poach for 4 minutes (add 30 seconds for firm yolks).

**4** Gently lift cooked eggs from water using slotted spoon and let drain before laying them on top of spinach. Season with salt and pepper to taste, and serve.

# overnight steel-cut oatmeal

serves 4

4 cups water

1 cup steel-cut oats

¼ teaspoon salt

Growing up, I was lucky enough to go to a great summer camp. We rode horses, learned archery and rifle skills, paddled canoes up and down the river, and sometimes slept right under the stars. But to get to those great parts of the day, we had to start each morning with the worst bowl of oatmeal ever. That stuff was so stodgy and slimy, it would pull the spoon back into the bowl on its own. So I know bad oatmeal. But this recipe, well, it's a game changer. The grains of oats are soft, but still a little chewy, and the whole mixture is creamy–almost luxurious. Do yourself a favor–start this recipe the night before, and enjoy a big bowl for breakfast. You'll feel as good as if you slept under the stars. "

*bridget*

1 Bring 3 cups water to boil in large saucepan over high heat. Remove pan from heat; stir in oats and salt. Cover pan and let stand overnight.

2 Stir remaining 1 cup water into oats and bring to boil over medium-high heat. Reduce heat to medium and cook, stirring occasionally, until oats are softened but still retain some chew and mixture thickens and resembles warm pudding, 4 to 6 minutes. Remove pan from heat and let stand for 5 minutes before serving.

*variations*

### apple-cinnamon overnight steel-cut oatmeal

Substitute ½ cup apple cider and ½ cup whole milk for water in step 2. Stir ½ cup grated peeled sweet apple, 2 tablespoons packed dark brown sugar, and ½ teaspoon ground cinnamon into oatmeal with cider and milk. Sprinkle individual portions with 2 tablespoons coarsely chopped toasted walnuts before serving.

### carrot spice overnight steel-cut oatmeal

Substitute ½ cup carrot juice and ½ cup whole milk for water in step 2. Stir ½ cup finely grated carrot, ¼ cup packed dark brown sugar, ⅓ cup dried currants, and ½ teaspoon ground cinnamon into oatmeal with carrot juice and milk.

Sprinkle individual portions with 2 tablespoons coarsely chopped toasted pecans before serving.

### peanut, honey, and banana overnight steel-cut oatmeal

Increase salt to ½ teaspoon. Substitute ½ cup whole milk for ½ cup water in step 2. Stir 3 tablespoons honey into oatmeal with milk and water. Add ¼ cup peanut butter and 1 tablespoon unsalted butter to oatmeal after removing from heat in step 2. Stir 2 bananas, cut into ½-inch pieces, into oatmeal. Sprinkle individual portions with 2 tablespoons coarsely chopped toasted peanuts before serving.

### banana-coconut overnight steel-cut oatmeal

Increase salt to ½ teaspoon. Substitute 1 cup canned coconut milk for water in step 2. Stir 2 bananas, cut into ½-inch pieces; ½ cup toasted shredded coconut; and ½ teaspoon vanilla extract into oatmeal before serving.

### cranberry-orange overnight steel-cut oatmeal

Substitute ½ cup orange juice and ½ cup whole milk for water in step 2. Stir ½ cup dried cranberries, 3 tablespoons packed dark brown sugar, and ⅛ teaspoon ground cardamom into oatmeal with orange juice and milk. Sprinkle individual portions with 2 tablespoons toasted sliced almonds before serving.

*Weekend Breakfasts*

# almond granola with dried fruit

makes about 9 cups

⅓ cup maple syrup

⅓ cup packed (2⅓ ounces) light brown sugar

4 teaspoons vanilla extract

½ teaspoon salt

½ cup vegetable oil

5 cups (15 ounces) old-fashioned rolled oats

2 cups (10 ounces) raw whole almonds, chopped coarse

2 cups raisins or other dried fruit, chopped

**1** Adjust oven rack to upper-middle position and heat oven to 325 degrees. Whisk maple syrup, sugar, vanilla, and salt in large bowl. Whisk in oil. Fold in oats and almonds until thoroughly coated.

**2** Transfer oat mixture to parchment paper–lined rimmed baking sheet and spread across sheet into thin, even layer (about ⅜ inch thick). Using stiff metal spatula, compress oat mixture until very compact. Bake until lightly browned, 40 to 45 minutes, rotating sheet halfway through baking.

**3** Remove granola from oven and let cool on baking sheet to room temperature, about 1 hour. Break cooled granola into pieces of desired size. Stir in raisins. (Granola can be stored at room temperature for up to 2 weeks.) Serve.

*variations*

### pecan-orange granola with dried cranberries

Add 2 tablespoons finely grated orange zest (2 oranges) and 2½ teaspoons ground cinnamon to maple syrup mixture in step 1. Substitute coarsely chopped pecans for almonds and dried cranberries for raisins.

### tropical granola with dried mango

Reduce vanilla to 2 teaspoons and add 1½ teaspoons ground ginger and ¾ teaspoon freshly grated nutmeg to maple syrup mixture in step 1. Substitute coarsely chopped macadamias for almonds, 1½ cups unsweetened shredded coconut for 1 cup oats, and chopped dried mango for raisins.

"

I was never a big fan of granola until this recipe came out of the test kitchen—it's downright amazing. Unlike other granolas, which need to be served with a little yogurt to add moisture or some fresh berries to add flavor, this stuff tastes great right out of hand. I love having this in the cupboard for snacking. Also, the recipe is surprisingly simple (just toss everything together and bake), with a relatively short ingredient list. I'm told that this granola will hold well for up to two weeks, but it disappears much faster than that in my house. "

*julia*

# avocado toast

serves 4

2 tablespoons extra-virgin olive oil

1 teaspoon finely grated lemon zest plus 1 tablespoon juice

Coarse sea salt or kosher salt and pepper

2 ripe avocados, halved and pitted (1 chopped, 1 sliced thin)

4 (⅔-inch-thick) slices crusty bread

¼ teaspoon red pepper flakes (optional)

"

When Marta was born, we started eating lots of avocados because they mashed so easily into baby food and were on all of the 'superfood' and 'brain food' lists I researched. So, when I smashed some up for her lunch, I usually swiped some onto a cracker or a piece of toast for myself. I never thought much about it until we developed this recipe for our vegetarian cookbook. Adding the lemon–olive oil mixture to the mashed avocado really kicks the flavor up a few notches and I love the contrasting texture of the mashed and sliced avocado. For breakfast, I often throw a fried egg or slices of hard-boiled egg over the top. "

*julia*

1  Whisk oil, lemon zest and juice, ¼ teaspoon salt, and ⅛ teaspoon pepper together in small bowl. Add chopped avocado and mash into dressing with fork.

2  Adjust oven rack 4 inches from broiler element and heat broiler. Place bread on aluminum foil–lined baking sheet. Broil until bread is deep golden on both sides, 1 to 2 minutes per side.

3  Spread mashed avocado mixture evenly on toasts. Arrange avocado slices evenly over top. Sprinkle with ¼ teaspoon salt and pepper flakes, if using, and serve.

# crispy potato latkes

serves 4 to 6

2 pounds russet potatoes, unpeeled, shredded

½ cup grated onion

Salt and pepper

2 large eggs, lightly beaten

2 teaspoons minced fresh parsley

Vegetable oil

1 Adjust oven rack to middle position and heat oven to 200 degrees. Toss potatoes with onion and 1 teaspoon salt in bowl. Working in 2 batches, wring potato mixture of excess moisture using clean dish towel over bowl; reserve drained liquid and transfer dried potatoes to clean bowl.

2 Cover potatoes and microwave until just warmed through but not hot, 1 to 2 minutes, stirring with fork every 30 seconds. Spread potatoes over baking sheet and let cool for 10 minutes; return to bowl.

3 Meanwhile, let bowl of drained potato liquid sit for 5 minutes so that starch can settle to bottom. Pour off liquid, leaving starch in bowl. Whisk eggs into starch until smooth. Add starch-egg mixture, parsley, and ¼ teaspoon pepper to cooled potatoes and toss gently to combine.

4 Add oil to 12-inch skillet until it measures ¼ inch deep. Heat oil over medium-high heat until shimmering but not smoking (about 350 degrees). Set wire rack in rimmed baking sheet and line with triple layer of paper towels.

5 Using ¼ cup potato mixture per latke, portion 5 latkes into hot skillet, pressing each into ⅓-inch-thick pancake. Cook until golden brown on both sides, about 6 minutes, adjusting heat as needed so that oil bubbles around edges of pancakes.

6 Transfer latkes to prepared baking sheet and keep warm in oven. Repeat with remaining potato mixture, adding oil as needed to maintain ¼-inch depth and returning oil to 350 degrees between batches. Season latkes with salt and pepper to taste, and serve.

# egg, ham, and hash brown pie

serves 4

⅓ cup olive oil

1 onion, chopped fine

½ teaspoon salt

½ teaspoon ground coriander

2 garlic cloves, minced

16 ounces (5 cups) frozen shredded hash browns, thawed

4 large eggs, lightly beaten

4 ounces Monterey Jack cheese, shredded (1 cup)

2 tablespoons minced fresh parsley

¼ teaspoon pepper

4 ounces ham steak, cut into ½-inch cubes

> This recipe was actually Ian's invention, which I then brought into the test kitchen and turned into a recipe. It's an easy riff on a traditional Spanish potato tortilla (which is another one of my favorite recipes; see page 24) but it includes cheese, ham, and crispy hash browns. This recipe calls for Monterey Jack, which tastes delicious, but we often swap in goat cheese. Also, you can easily substitute sausage or other types of deli meat (such as corned beef or pastrami) for the ham. It's important to choose the right brand of hash browns for this or they won't brown well; I prefer to use Alexia brand all natural frozen hashed browns. Be sure to save some for leftovers for breakfast or lunch the next day; it tastes terrific cold.

*julia*

1  Cook oil, onion, salt, and coriander in 10-inch nonstick skillet over medium-high heat until onion is softened, about 5 minutes. Stir in garlic and cook until fragrant, about 30 seconds. Stir in hash browns and cook, stirring often, until potatoes are crisp and brown, about 10 minutes.

2  Whisk eggs, Monterey Jack, parsley, and pepper together in large bowl, then stir in ham and cooked potato mixture. Pour mixture into now-empty skillet and cook over medium-high heat, gently shaking pan occasionally, until bottom is golden and top is lightly set, about 5 minutes.

3  Off heat, run heatproof rubber spatula around edge of pan and shake pan gently to loosen pie; it should slide around freely in pan. Slide pie onto large plate, then invert onto second large plate and slide back into skillet browned side up. Continue to cook over medium heat until second side is golden and eggs are cooked through, about 2 minutes. Slide pie onto cutting board and let cool slightly before serving.

# short-order home fries

serves 4

1½ pounds Yukon Gold potatoes, unpeeled, cut into ¾-inch pieces

4 tablespoons unsalted butter

1 onion, chopped fine

½ teaspoon garlic salt

Salt and pepper

"Before we had kids, my husband and I lived in Boston's North End–also known as Boston's Little Italy. Though there was no shortage of great Italian food, we loved eating once a weekend at a little diner called the Freedom Trail, which was around the corner from our apartment. The breakfast cook was a magician, and it was great to watch the speed and accuracy with which he delivered the hot breakfast food to the customers. But the best part was the home fries, crisp, tender, and seasoned with garlic salt. Just like this version. By the way, you can microwave the potatoes as well as cook the onions and then refrigerate both mixtures overnight. That way all you need to do in the morning is heat some butter, pack in the mixture, and cook until it's browned."

*bridget*

1 Place potatoes and 1 tablespoon butter in large bowl and microwave, covered, until edges of potatoes begin to soften, 5 to 7 minutes, stirring halfway through microwaving.

2 Meanwhile, melt 1 tablespoon butter in 12-inch nonstick skillet over medium heat. Add onion and cook until softened and golden brown, 8 to 10 minutes. Transfer to small bowl.

3 Melt remaining 2 tablespoons butter in now-empty skillet over medium heat. Add potatoes and pack down with spatula. Cook, without moving, until bottoms of potatoes are brown, 5 to 7 minutes. Turn potatoes, pack down again, and continue to cook until well browned and crisp, 5 to 7 minutes. Reduce heat to medium-low and continue to cook until potatoes are crusty, 9 to 12 minutes, stirring occasionally. Stir in onion, garlic salt, ½ teaspoon salt, and pepper to taste. Serve.

# nectarine, grape, and blueberry fruit salad with orange and cardamom

serves 4 to 6

4 teaspoons sugar

1 teaspoon grated orange zest

⅛ teaspoon ground cardamom

1½ pounds nectarines, halved, pitted, and cut into ½-inch pieces

9 ounces large green grapes, halved (about 1½ cups)

10 ounces (2 cups) blueberries

1-2 tablespoons lime juice

Combine sugar, orange zest, and cardamom in large bowl. Using rubber spatula, press mixture into side of bowl until sugar becomes damp, about 30 seconds. Gently toss fruit with sugar mixture until combined. Let stand at room temperature, stirring occasionally, until fruit releases its juices, 15 to 30 minutes. Stir in lime juice to taste, and serve.

### variations
### cantaloupe, plum, and cherry fruit salad with mint and vanilla

4 teaspoons sugar

1-2 tablespoons minced fresh mint

¼ teaspoon vanilla extract

3 cups cantaloupe, cut into ½-inch pieces

2 plums, halved, pitted, and cut into ½-inch pieces

8 ounces fresh sweet cherries, pitted and halved

1-2 tablespoons lime juice

Combine sugar and mint to taste in large bowl. Using rubber spatula, press mixture into side of bowl until sugar becomes damp, about 30 seconds; add vanilla. Gently toss fruit with sugar mixture until combined. Let sit at room temperature, stirring occasionally, until fruit releases its juices, 15 to 30 minutes. Stir in lime juice to taste, and serve.

### honeydew, mango, and raspberry fruit salad with lime and ginger

4 teaspoons sugar

2 teaspoons grated lime zest plus 1-2 tablespoons juice

Pinch cayenne pepper (optional)

3 cups honeydew melon, cut into ½-inch pieces

1 mango, peeled, pitted, and cut into ½-inch pieces

1-2 teaspoons grated fresh ginger

5 ounces (1 cup) raspberries

Combine sugar, lime zest, and cayenne, if using, in large bowl. Using rubber spatula, press mixture into side of bowl until sugar becomes damp, about 30 seconds. Gently toss honeydew, mango, and ginger to taste with sugar mixture until combined. Let sit at room temperature, stirring occasionally, until fruit releases its juices, 15 to 30 minutes. Gently stir in raspberries. Stir in lime juice to taste, and serve.

## peach, blackberry, and strawberry fruit salad with basil and pepper

4 teaspoons sugar

2 tablespoons chopped fresh basil

½ teaspoon pepper

1½ pounds peaches, halved, pitted, and cut into ½-inch pieces

10 ounces (2 cups) blackberries

10 ounces strawberries, hulled and quartered lengthwise (2 cups)

1–2 tablespoons lime juice

Combine sugar, basil, and pepper in large bowl. Using rubber spatula, press mixture into side of bowl until sugar becomes damp, about 30 seconds. Gently toss fruit with sugar mixture until combined. Let sit at room temperature, stirring occasionally, until fruit releases its juices, 15 to 30 minutes. Stir in lime juice to taste, and serve.

# cat head biscuits

makes 6 biscuits

1½ cups (7½ ounces) all-purpose flour

1½ cups (6 ounces) cake flour

1 tablespoon baking powder

½ teaspoon baking soda

1 teaspoon salt

8 tablespoons unsalted butter, cut into ½-inch pieces and softened

4 tablespoons vegetable shortening, cut into ½-inch pieces

1¼ cups buttermilk

'We should do "cat head" biscuits,' I said to the *Cook's Country* magazine test cooks. They looked at me like I had two heads, which is pretty relevant, since cat head biscuits are B-I-G! As big as a cat's head, they say. This type of biscuit is pretty common in the Appalachian area where I was raised, and there you'll see as many biscuit sandwich restaurants as you do fast-food joints. You bake this type of biscuit in a pan and space the portions of dough close together. As the biscuits bake, they snuggle together and then rise straight up. The result is biscuits with rough, craggy tops and soft-as-a-pillow sides. Purrfect, especially when I use lard instead of Crisco.

*bridget*

1 Adjust oven rack to upper-middle position and heat oven to 425 degrees. Grease 9-inch cake pan. Whisk all-purpose flour, cake flour, baking powder, baking soda, and salt together in large bowl. Rub butter and shortening into flour mixture until mixture resembles coarse meal. Stir in buttermilk until combined.

2 Using greased ½-cup dry measuring cup or large spring-loaded ice cream scoop, transfer 6 heaping portions dough to prepared pan, placing five around pan's perimeter and one in center.

3 Bake until puffed and golden brown, 20 to 25 minutes, rotating pan halfway through baking. Let biscuits cool in pan for 10 minutes, then transfer to wire rack. Serve. (Biscuits can be stored in airtight container at room temperature for up to 2 days.)

# ultimate banana bread

makes 1 loaf

> ❝
> I never ate banana bread as a kid (my mother didn't like having bread or sugary things around) and today I still consider it a real treat, which is why I like this recipe. This bread is more than just a tasty way to use up an old banana or two (my old bananas go into the freezer for making smoothies anyway), but rather highlights the flavor of six (yes, six!) perfectly over-ripe bananas. The key to this recipe's intense banana flavor is microwaving the bananas to get them to release their liquid. This banana juice then gets reduced and added back to the batter separately. You have to plan ahead for this recipe and let the bananas sit on the counter until they are nearly all black, which can take up to a week, but it's well worth the wait. ❞

*julia*

1¾ cups (8¾ ounces) all-purpose flour

1 teaspoon baking soda

½ teaspoon salt

6 very ripe large bananas (2¼ pounds), peeled

8 tablespoons unsalted butter, melted and cooled

2 large eggs

¾ cup packed (5¼ ounces) light brown sugar

1 teaspoon vanilla extract

½ cup walnuts, toasted and chopped coarse (optional)

2 teaspoons granulated sugar

1   Adjust oven rack to middle position and heat oven to 350 degrees. Grease 8½ by 4½-inch loaf pan. Whisk flour, baking soda, and salt together in large bowl.

2   Place 5 bananas in separate bowl, cover, and microwave until bananas are soft and have released liquid, about 5 minutes. Drain bananas in fine-mesh strainer set over medium bowl, stirring occasionally, for 15 minutes; you should have ½ to ¾ cup liquid.

3   Transfer drained liquid to medium saucepan and cook over medium-high heat until reduced to ¼ cup, about 5 minutes. Return drained bananas to bowl. Stir reduced liquid into bananas and mash with potato masher until mostly smooth. Whisk in melted butter, eggs, brown sugar, and vanilla.

4   Pour banana mixture into flour mixture and stir until just combined, with some streaks of flour remaining. Gently fold in walnuts, if using. Scrape batter into prepared loaf pan and smooth top. Slice remaining 1 banana on bias into ¼-inch-thick slices and shingle down both sides of loaf pan, leaving center clear to ensure even rise. Sprinkle granulated sugar over top.

5   Bake until skewer inserted in center comes out clean, 55 minutes to 1¼ hours, rotating pan halfway through baking. Let loaf cool in pan for 15 minutes, then turn out onto wire rack and continue to cool. Serve warm or at room temperature.

# monkey bread

serves 6 to 8

### dough

3¼ cups (16¼ ounces) all-purpose flour

2¼ teaspoons instant or rapid-rise yeast

2 teaspoons salt

1 cup whole milk, room temperature

⅓ cup water, room temperature

¼ cup (1¾ ounces) granulated sugar

2 tablespoons unsalted butter, melted

### brown sugar coating

1 cup packed (7 ounces) light brown sugar

2 teaspoons ground cinnamon

8 tablespoons unsalted butter, melted and cooled

### glaze

1 cup (4 ounces) confectioners' sugar

2 tablespoons whole milk

> My grandpa was a great cook, and he always shared recipes with my mom to make for our family. One of his favorite tricks was taking homemade biscuit dough and turning it into something else—like monkey bread. We kids would take turns rolling the dough into balls, dipping them into butter, then sugar and cinnamon, and finally stacking the balls into a tube pan. Once it was baked, we'd pull apart the pieces of monkey bread like ravenous gorillas. These days I make this yeast-dough version with my own little monkeys.
>
> *bridget*

1  **For the dough**  Whisk flour, yeast, and salt together in bowl of stand mixer. Whisk milk, water, sugar, and melted butter in 4-cup liquid measuring cup until sugar has dissolved. Using dough hook on low speed, slowly add milk mixture to flour mixture and mix until cohesive dough starts to form and no dry flour remains, about 2 minutes, scraping down bowl as needed. Increase speed to medium-low and knead until dough is smooth and elastic and clears sides of bowl but sticks to bottom, 8 to 10 minutes.

2  Transfer dough to lightly floured counter and knead by hand to form smooth, round ball, about 30 seconds. Place dough seam side down in lightly greased large bowl or container, cover tightly with plastic wrap, and let rise until doubled in size, 1½ to 2 hours. (Unrisen dough can be refrigerated for at least 8 hours or up to 16 hours; let sit at room temperature for 1 hour before shaping in step 4.)

3  **For the brown sugar coating**  Thoroughly grease 12-cup nonstick Bundt pan. Combine sugar and cinnamon in medium bowl. Place melted butter in second bowl.

**4** Transfer dough to lightly floured counter and press into rough 8-inch square. Using pizza cutter or chef's knife, cut dough into 8 even strips. Cut each strip into 8 pieces (64 pieces total). Cover loosely with greased plastic.

**5** Working with a few pieces of dough at a time (keep remaining pieces covered), place on clean counter and, using your cupped hand, drag in small circles until dough feels taut and round. Dip balls in melted butter, then roll in sugar mixture to coat. Place balls in prepared pan, staggering seams where dough balls meet as you build layers.

**6** Cover pan tightly with plastic and let rise until dough balls reach 1 to 2 inches below lip of pan, 1 ½ to 2 hours.

**7** Adjust oven rack to middle position and heat oven to 350 degrees. Bake until top is deep golden brown and caramel begins to bubble around edges, 30 to 35 minutes. Let bread cool in pan for 5 minutes, then invert onto serving platter and let cool for 10 minutes.

**8** **For the glaze** Meanwhile, whisk sugar and milk in bowl until smooth. Drizzle glaze over bread, letting it run down sides. Serve warm.

# pumpkin bread

makes 2 loaves

> Whereas banana bread only makes special appearances at my house, pumpkin bread is often on hand because it is Ian and Marta's favorite snack. I've tried various recipes over the years and landed on this version as the best because the pumpkin puree gets cooked down on the stovetop, which intensifies the pumpkin flavor. I also like the rich (but not greasy) texture that the cream cheese adds. I often omit the topping for the sake of ease, although the bread definitely tastes better with it. Also, I rarely make two loaves, but rather make one loaf for Ian and turn the rest of the batter into mini muffins for Marta. Mini muffins freeze very well and thaw quickly when left on the counter for about an hour. 99

*julia*

### topping

5 tablespoons packed (2¼ ounces) light brown sugar

1 tablespoon all-purpose flour

1 tablespoon unsalted butter, softened

1 teaspoon ground cinnamon

⅛ teaspoon salt

### bread

2 cups (10 ounces) all-purpose flour

1½ teaspoons baking powder

½ teaspoon baking soda

1 (15-ounce) can unsweetened pumpkin puree

1½ teaspoons ground cinnamon

1 teaspoon salt

¼ teaspoon ground nutmeg

⅛ teaspoon ground cloves

1 cup (7 ounces) granulated sugar

1 cup packed (7 ounces) light brown sugar

½ cup vegetable oil

4 ounces cream cheese, cut into 12 pieces

4 large eggs

¼ cup buttermilk

1 cup walnuts, toasted and chopped fine

**1 For the topping** Using your fingers, mix all ingredients in bowl until well combined and mixture resembles wet sand.

**2 For the bread** Adjust oven rack to middle position and heat oven to 350 degrees. Grease two 8½ by 4½-inch loaf pans. Whisk flour, baking powder, and baking soda together in bowl.

**3** Cook pumpkin puree, cinnamon, salt, nutmeg, and cloves in large saucepan over medium heat, stirring constantly, until reduced to 1½ cups, 6 to 8 minutes. Off heat, stir in granulated sugar, brown sugar, oil, and cream cheese until combined. Let mixture stand for 5 minutes. Whisk until no visible pieces of cream cheese remain and mixture is homogeneous.

**4** Whisk eggs and buttermilk together in separate bowl, then whisk into pumpkin mixture. Gently fold in flour mixture until combined (some small lumps of flour are OK). Fold in walnuts. Scrape batter into prepared pans, smooth tops, and sprinkle evenly with topping. Bake until skewer inserted in center comes out clean, 45 to 50 minutes, rotating pans halfway through baking.

**5** Let loaves cool in pans for 20 minutes, then turn out onto wire rack and let cool for 1½ hours before serving.

# ultimate cinnamon buns

makes 8 buns

"

We were driving down to the Outer Banks for a family vacation and we stopped in Virginia, at one of those mega gas stations, to fuel up and stretch our legs. Inside the station was a Cinnabon (if I hadn't spotted it I could have smelled that incredible cinnamon aroma a mile away). My kids had never had Cinnabon, so I picked up a package of six for the road for all of us to share. Let me tell you, everything that's great about a Cinnabon roll—the big size, the gooey cinnamon sugar filling, and the creamy cream cheese frosting— makes it a nightmare on a road trip. Our kids' gooey hands were every- where, and I was cleaning sticky stuff off the seats, floor, and ceiling of the car for weeks. Luckily for me, I can make this awesome version at home and keep those sticky fingers contained to the kitchen table. "

*bridget*

### dough

¾ cup whole milk (110 degrees)

2¼ teaspoons instant or rapid-rise yeast

3 large eggs, room temperature

4¼-4½ cups (21¼ to 22½ ounces) all-purpose flour

½ cup (2 ounces) cornstarch

½ cup (3½ ounces) granulated sugar

1½ teaspoons salt

12 tablespoons unsalted butter, cut into 12 pieces and softened

### filling

1½ cups packed (10½ ounces) light brown sugar

1½ tablespoons ground cinnamon

¼ teaspoon salt

4 tablespoons unsalted butter, softened

### glaze

1½ cups (6 ounces) confectioners' sugar

4 ounces cream cheese, softened

1 tablespoon whole milk

1 teaspoon vanilla extract

1  **For the dough**  Make foil sling for 13 by 9-inch baking pan by folding 2 long sheets of aluminum foil; first sheet should be 13 inches wide and second sheet should be 9 inches wide. Lay sheets of foil in pan perpen- dicular to each other, with extra foil hanging over edges of pan. Push foil into corners and up sides of pan, smoothing foil flush to pan. Grease foil.

2  Whisk milk and yeast together in liquid measuring cup until yeast dissolves, then whisk in eggs. Combine 4¼ cups flour, cornstarch, sugar, and salt in bowl of stand mixer. Using dough hook on low speed, slowly add milk mixture and mix until dough comes together, about 1 minute. Increase speed to medium and add butter, 1 piece at a time, until incor- porated. Continue to mix until dough is smooth and comes away from sides of bowl, about 10 minutes. (If after 5 minutes more flour is needed, add remaining ¼ cup flour, 1 tablespoon at a time, until dough clears sides of bowl but sticks to bottom.)

3  Transfer dough to lightly floured counter and knead by hand to form smooth, round ball, about 1 minute. Place dough in lightly greased large bowl, cover tightly with greased plastic wrap, and let rise until doubled in size, about 2 hours.

**4 For the filling** Combine sugar, cinnamon, and salt in bowl. Transfer dough to lightly floured counter and roll into 18-inch square. Spread butter over dough, leaving ½-inch border at edges. Sprinkle with filling, leaving ¾-inch border at top edge, and press lightly to adhere. Roll dough away from you into firm cylinder, keeping roll taut by tucking it under itself as you go. Pinch seam closed. Using serrated knife, cut cylinder into 8 pieces and arrange, cut side down, in prepared pan. Cover with plastic and let rise until doubled in size, about 1 hour.

**5** Adjust oven rack to middle position and heat oven to 350 degrees. Bake until buns are deep golden brown and filling is melted, 35 to 40 minutes, rotating pan halfway through baking.

**6 For the glaze** Whisk all ingredients together in bowl until smooth. Drizzle glaze over buns as soon as they come out of oven. Let glazed buns cool in pan for 30 minutes, then remove from pan using sling and serve.

# sour cream coffee cake
# with brown sugar–pecan streusel

serves 12 to 16

### streusel

¾ cup (3¾ ounces) all-purpose flour

¾ cup (5¼ ounces) granulated sugar

½ cup packed (3½ ounces) dark brown sugar

2 tablespoons ground cinnamon

2 tablespoons unsalted butter, cut into 2 pieces and chilled

1 cup pecans, chopped

### cake

12 tablespoons unsalted butter, cut into ½-inch cubes and softened but still cool, plus 2 tablespoons softened for greasing pan

4 large eggs

1½ cups sour cream

1 tablespoon vanilla extract

2¼ cups (11¼ ounces) all-purpose flour

1¼ cups (8¾ ounces) granulated sugar

1 tablespoon baking powder

¾ teaspoon baking soda

¾ teaspoon salt

1  **For the streusel**  Process flour, granulated sugar, ¼ cup brown sugar, and cinnamon in food processor until combined, about 15 seconds. Transfer 1¼ cups of flour-sugar mixture to small bowl and stir in remaining ¼ cup brown sugar; set aside for streusel filling. Add butter and pecans to mixture in food processor and pulse until nuts and butter resemble small pebbly pieces, about 10 pulses. Set aside for streusel topping.

2  **For the cake**  Adjust oven rack to lowest position and heat oven to 350 degrees. Grease and flour 10-inch tube pan with 2 tablespoons softened butter. Whisk eggs, 1 cup sour cream, and vanilla in medium bowl until combined.

3  Using stand mixer fitted with paddle, mix flour, sugar, baking powder, baking soda, and salt on low speed for 30 seconds to combine. Add remaining 12 tablespoons butter and remaining ½ cup sour cream and mix until dry ingredients are moistened and mixture resembles wet sand, with few large butter pieces remaining, about 1½ minutes. Increase speed to medium and beat until batter comes together,

about 10 seconds; scrape down sides of bowl with rubber spatula. Lower speed to medium-low and gradually add egg mixture in 3 additions, beating for 20 seconds after each and scraping down sides of bowl. Increase speed to medium-high and beat until batter is light and fluffy, about 1 minute.

**4** Using rubber spatula, spread 2 cups batter in bottom of prepared pan and smooth surface. Sprinkle evenly with ¾ cup streusel filling. Repeat with another 2 cups batter and remaining ¾ cup streusel filling. Spread remaining batter over filling, then sprinkle with streusel topping.

**5** Bake until cake feels firm to touch and skewer inserted in center comes out clean (bits of sugar from streusel may cling to skewer), 50 minutes to 1 hour, rotating pan halfway through baking. Let cake cool in pan on wire rack for 30 minutes. Gently invert cake onto rimmed baking sheet (cake will be streusel side down); remove tube pan, place wire rack on top of cake, and invert cake streusel side up. Let cool to room temperature, about 2 hours, before serving.

# home-style dinners

# one-pan roasted chicken with root vegetables

serves 4

"

We make this recipe at least twice a month at our house. I love that it's a healthy one-pan meal with a lot of colorful vegetables. We can't get my daughter to eat the potatoes or shallots yet, but she goes nuts for the Brussels sprouts–go figure! The Brussels sprouts do taste terrific because during cooking they're protected in the center of the pan with the chicken on top and essentially get basted with delicious chicken schmaltz the entire time. Also, I've found that the tray can be fully prepped and refrigerated overnight. This a great time-saver when our schedules get busy, and it is a great thing to drop off at a friend's house (with roasting instructions) when they need a helping hand. "

*julia*

12 ounces Brussels sprouts, trimmed and halved

12 ounces red potatoes, unpeeled, cut into 1-inch pieces

8 shallots, peeled and halved lengthwise

4 carrots, peeled and cut into 2-inch lengths, thick ends halved lengthwise

6 garlic cloves, peeled

1 tablespoon vegetable oil

4 teaspoons minced fresh thyme or 1½ teaspoons dried

2 teaspoons minced fresh rosemary or ¾ teaspoon dried

1 teaspoon sugar

Salt and pepper

2 tablespoons unsalted butter, melted

3½ pounds bone-in chicken pieces (2 split breasts cut in half crosswise, 2 drumsticks, and 2 thighs), trimmed

1 Adjust oven rack to upper-middle position and heat oven to 475 degrees. Toss Brussels sprouts, potatoes, shallots, carrots, garlic, oil, 2 teaspoons thyme, 1 teaspoon rosemary, sugar, ¾ teaspoon salt, and ¼ teaspoon pepper together in bowl. Combine melted butter, remaining 2 teaspoons thyme, remaining 1 teaspoon rosemary, ¼ teaspoon salt, and ⅛ teaspoon pepper in second bowl. Pat chicken dry with paper towels and season with salt and pepper.

2 Place vegetables in single layer on rimmed baking sheet, arranging Brussels sprouts in center. Place chicken, skin side up, on top of vegetables, arranging breast pieces in center and thighs and drumsticks around perimeter of sheet. Brush chicken with herb butter. Roast until breasts register 160 degrees and drumsticks/thighs register 175 degrees, 35 to 40 minutes, rotating pan half-way through roasting.

3 Remove sheet from oven, tent with aluminum foil, and let rest for 5 minutes. Transfer chicken to platter. Toss vegetables with pan juices, season with salt and pepper to taste, and transfer to platter. Serve.

*variation*

## one-pan roasted chicken with fennel and parsnips

Substitute 1 fennel bulb, stalks discarded, bulb halved, cored, and sliced into ½-inch wedges, for Brussels sprouts, and 8 ounces parsnips, peeled and cut into 2-inch pieces, for carrots.

# grilled butterflied lemon chicken

serves 8

2 (4-pound) whole chickens, giblets discarded

5 lemons

Salt and pepper

1 (13 by 9-inch) disposable aluminum pan (if using charcoal)

1 garlic clove, minced

2 tablespoons minced fresh parsley

2 teaspoons Dijon mustard

1 teaspoon sugar

⅔ cup extra-virgin olive oil

"

Sure, this recipe produces juicy, herbal chicken, and quickly too (thanks, butterflying!), but it also includes a trick that I use just about any time that I grill food: Halve some lemons (or limes or oranges) and place them cut side down on the grill. The flesh will char just a bit, and the citrus juice will deepen in flavor. Go ahead and squeeze the grilled lemons on just about anything and tell me it's not amazing. "

*bridget*

1  Set wire rack in rimmed baking sheet. Working with 1 chicken at a time, place chicken breast side down on cutting board. Using kitchen shears, cut through bones on either side of backbone; discard backbone. Trim chicken of excess fat and skin. Flip chicken over and press on breastbone to flatten. Cover chicken with plastic wrap and pound breasts with meat pounder to even thickness.

2  Grate 2 teaspoons zest from 1 lemon (halve and reserve lemon) and mix with 2 teaspoons salt and 1 teaspoon pepper in bowl. Pat chickens dry with paper towels and, using your fingers or handle of wooden spoon, gently loosen skin covering breasts and thighs. Rub zest mixture under skin, then season exterior of chickens with salt and pepper. Tuck wingtips behind breasts and transfer chickens to prepared rack. Refrigerate, uncovered, for at least 1 hour or up to 24 hours.

3A  For a charcoal grill  Open bottom vent completely and place disposable pan on 1 side of grill with long side of pan facing center of grill. Light large chimney starter filled with charcoal briquettes (6 quarts). When top coals are partially covered with ash, pour evenly over other half of grill (opposite disposable pan). Scatter 20 unlit coals on top of lit coals. Set cooking grate in place, cover, and open lid vent completely. Heat grill until hot, about 5 minutes.

3B  For a gas grill  Turn all burners to high, cover, and heat grill until hot, about 15 minutes. Leave primary burner on high and turn other burner(s) to low. (Adjust primary burner as needed to maintain grill temperature of 350 to 375 degrees.)

4  Clean and oil cooking grate. Halve remaining 4 lemons and place, along with reserved lemon halves, cut side down on hotter side of grill. Place chickens skin side down on cooler side of grill, with legs pointing toward fire; cover, placing lid vent over chickens on charcoal grill.

5  Grill lemons until deep brown and caramelized, 5 to 8 minutes; transfer to bowl. Continue to grill chickens, covered, until breasts register 160 degrees and thighs register 175 degrees, 40 to 50 minutes longer. Slide chickens to hotter side of grill and cook, uncovered, until skin is well browned, 2 to 4 minutes.

Transfer chickens to carving board skin side up, tent with aluminum foil, and let rest for 15 minutes.

**6** Meanwhile, squeeze $\frac{1}{3}$ cup juice from grilled lemons into bowl. (Cut any unsqueezed lemons into wedges for serving.) Using flat side of knife, mash garlic and $\frac{1}{2}$ teaspoon salt into paste and add to bowl with lemon juice. Whisk in parsley, mustard, sugar, and $\frac{1}{2}$ teaspoon pepper. Slowly whisk in oil until emulsified.

**7** Carve chickens, transfer to serving platter, and pour $\frac{1}{3}$ cup vinaigrette over chicken. Serve, passing remaining vinaigrette and grilled lemon wedges separately.

# alabama barbecue chicken

serves 4 to 6

True story: I'm addicted to mayonnaise. I even mail-order my favorite brand (Duke's) since I can't buy it up here in the Northeast. Deviled eggs–love them. Creamy dips–I'm in. So to hear of a barbecue sauce that uses mayo instead of ketchup or vinegar as its base? Sold! Seriously, you know when barbecued meat sidles up a little too closely to the creamy potato salad on your picnic plate? And the creamy dressing starts to meld with the smoke and spice on the meat? And how the combination is a perfect symphony of silky mayo goodness and smoky, succulent meat? Yep–that's this recipe. Make it now. "

*bridget*

### sauce

¾ cup mayonnaise

2 tablespoons cider vinegar

2 teaspoons sugar

½ teaspoon prepared horseradish

½ teaspoon salt

½ teaspoon black pepper

¼ teaspoon cayenne pepper

### chicken

1 teaspoon salt

1 teaspoon black pepper

½ teaspoon cayenne pepper

2 (3½- to 4-pound) whole chickens

2 cups wood chips, soaked in water for 15 minutes and drained

1 (13 by 9-inch) disposable aluminum roasting pan (if using charcoal)

**1  For the sauce**  Process ingredients in blender until smooth, about 1 minute. Refrigerate for at least 1 hour or up to 2 days.

**2  For the chicken**  Combine salt, pepper, and cayenne in small bowl. Working with 1 chicken at a time, place chicken breast side down on cutting board. Using kitchen shears, cut through bones on either side of backbone; discard backbone.

Trim chicken of excess fat and skin. Flip chicken over and, using chef's knife, cut through breastbone to separate chicken into halves. Pat chickens dry with paper towels and rub them evenly with spice mixture. Using large piece of heavy-duty aluminum foil, wrap soaked chips in 8 by 4½-inch foil packet. (Make sure chips do not poke holes in sides or bottom of packet.) Cut 2 evenly spaced 2-inch slits in top of packet.

**3A  For a charcoal grill**  Open bottom vent halfway and place disposable pan in center of grill. Light large chimney starter filled with charcoal briquettes (6 quarts). When top coals are partially covered with ash, pour into 2 even piles on either side of pan. Place wood chip packet on 1 pile of coals. Set cooking grate in place, cover, and open lid vent halfway. Heat grill until hot and wood chips are smoking, about 5 minutes.

**3B  For a gas grill**  Place wood chip packet directly on primary burner. Turn all burners to high, cover, and heat grill until hot and wood chips are smoking, about 15 minutes. Turn all burners to medium-low. (Adjust burners as needed to maintain grill temperature around 350 degrees.)

**4** Clean and oil cooking grate. Place chickens skin side down on grill (in center of grill if using charcoal). Cover (positioning lid vent over chickens if using charcoal) and cook chickens until well browned on bottom and thighs register 120 degrees, 35 to 45 minutes.

**5** Flip chickens skin side up. Cover and continue to cook chickens until skin is golden brown and crisp and breasts register 160 degrees and thighs register 175 degrees, 15 to 20 minutes longer.

**6** Transfer chickens to carving board and brush with 2 tablespoons sauce. Tent chickens with foil and let rest for 10 minutes. Brush chickens with remaining sauce, carve, and serve.

# classic chicken and rice with carrots and peas

serves 4

"

My family loves rice (more than potatoes or pasta), so this weeknight recipe is in heavy rotation at our house. I've tasted a number of chicken and rice recipes in the test kitchen over the years, but this version is my favorite because it uses long-grain rice and boneless chicken breasts, both of which are staples in my kitchen. Plus, this recipe comes together in about an hour. I've also found it to be very sturdy and easy to adapt. For example, I like adding various spices to the pan with the onions (smoked paprika, garam masala), swapping other vegetables for the carrots and peas (mushrooms, baby kale, and edamame), and cutting the broth with other flavorful liquids (coconut milk, dry vermouth). I use a straight-sided sauté pan because the skillet gets very full when you add the browned chicken. "

*julia*

4 (6- to 8-ounce) boneless, skinless chicken breasts, trimmed

Salt and pepper

2 tablespoons vegetable oil

1 onion, chopped fine

1½ cups long-grain white rice

3 garlic cloves, minced

Pinch red pepper flakes

4 carrots, peeled and sliced on bias ½ inch thick

3½ cups chicken broth

1 cup frozen peas

2 tablespoons lemon juice

1 tablespoon minced fresh parsley

1  Pat chicken dry with paper towels and season with salt and pepper. Heat oil in 12-inch skillet over medium-high heat until just smoking. Add chicken and cook until golden brown on 1 side, 4 to 6 minutes; transfer to plate.

2  Add onion and ½ teaspoon salt to fat left in skillet and cook until softened, about 5 minutes. Stir in rice, garlic, and pepper flakes and cook until fragrant, about 30 seconds. Stir in carrots, then stir in broth, scraping up any browned bits.

3  Nestle chicken, browned side up, into skillet, along with any accumulated juices. Bring to simmer, then reduce heat to medium-low, cover, and simmer gently until chicken registers 160 degrees, about 10 minutes.

4  Transfer chicken to cutting board, tent with aluminum foil, and let rest while finishing rice. Stir rice mixture to recombine, then cover and cook until liquid is absorbed and rice is tender, 5 to 10 minutes.

5  Off heat, sprinkle with peas, cover, and let warm through, about 2 minutes. Sprinkle with lemon juice and gently fluff rice mixture with fork. Slice chicken into ½-inch-thick slices and arrange on top of rice. Sprinkle with parsley and serve.

# no-fuss risotto with chicken and herbs

serves 6

"

Before this recipe came along, I didn't make risotto at home because it never felt like enough for dinner and the constant stirring required by most recipes is too much of a hassle for a weeknight. But this easy recipe is a game changer with its hands-off method and the addition of chicken. I often also throw in some vegetables, like carrots, fennel, and spinach, because if I put vegetables in everything I cook my family will eventually eat them. "

*julia*

5 cups chicken broth

2 cups water

1 tablespoon olive oil

2 (12-ounce) bone-in split chicken breasts, trimmed and halved crosswise

4 tablespoons unsalted butter

1 large onion, chopped fine

Salt and pepper

1 garlic clove, minced

2 cups Arborio rice

1 cup dry white wine

2 ounces Parmesan cheese, grated (1 cup)

2 tablespoons chopped fresh parsley

2 tablespoons chopped fresh chives

1 teaspoon lemon juice

1  Bring broth and water to boil in large saucepan over high heat. Reduce heat to medium-low to maintain gentle simmer.

2  Heat oil in Dutch oven over medium heat until just smoking. Add chicken skin side down and cook without moving it until golden brown, 4 to 6 minutes. Flip chicken and cook second side until lightly browned, about 2 minutes. Transfer chicken to saucepan and simmer until chicken registers 160 degrees, 10 to 15 minutes. Transfer to large plate.

3  Melt 2 tablespoons butter in now-empty Dutch oven over medium heat. Add onion and ¾ teaspoon salt and cook, stirring frequently, until onion is softened, 5 to 7 minutes. Add garlic and stir until fragrant, about 30 seconds. Add rice and cook, stirring frequently, until grains are translucent around edges, about 3 minutes.

4  Add wine and cook, stirring constantly, until fully absorbed, 2 to 3 minutes. Stir 5 cups hot broth mixture into rice; reduce heat to medium-low, cover, and simmer until almost all liquid has been absorbed and rice is just al dente, 16 to 19 minutes, stirring twice during cooking.

5  Add ¾ cup hot broth mixture and stir gently and constantly until risotto becomes creamy, about 3 minutes. Stir in Parmesan. Remove pot from heat, cover, and let stand for 5 minutes.

6  Meanwhile, shred chicken into bite-size pieces, discarding skin and bones. Gently stir shredded chicken, remaining 2 tablespoons butter, parsley, chives, and lemon juice into risotto. To loosen texture of risotto, add remaining hot broth mixture as needed. Season with salt and pepper to taste, and serve immediately.

# french chicken in a pot

serves 4

1 (4½- to 5-pound) whole chicken, giblets discarded

2 teaspoons kosher salt

¼ teaspoon pepper

1 tablespoon olive oil

1 small onion, chopped

1 small celery rib, chopped

6 garlic cloves, peeled

1 bay leaf

1 sprig fresh rosemary (optional)

½–1 teaspoon lemon juice

"

I remember making a few roast chickens for a family event, and working extra-hard to ensure that the meat was juicy and tender, and the skin was supercrisp. I served the chicken and watched as most of the folks at the table removed the skin from the meat and put it on the side of their plate–ready to be discarded. What a forehead-slapping moment! Roast chicken doesn't have to be all about the skin. That's why I love this recipe; the emphasis is solely on producing succulent, tender meat with a pan jus that is unadulterated chicken essence. "

*bridget*

1  Adjust oven rack to lowest position and heat oven to 250 degrees. Pat chicken dry with paper towels, tuck wings behind back, and sprinkle with salt and pepper. Heat oil in Dutch oven over medium heat until just smoking. Add chicken, breast side down, and scatter onion, celery, garlic, bay leaf, and rosemary sprig, if using, around chicken. Cook until breast is lightly browned, about 5 minutes. Using wooden spoon inserted into cavity of chicken, flip chicken breast side up and cook until chicken and vegetables are well browned, 6 to 8 minutes.

2  Off heat, place large sheet of aluminum foil over pot and cover tightly with lid. Transfer pot to oven and cook chicken until breast registers 160 degrees and thighs register 175 degrees, 1 hour 20 minutes to 1 hour 50 minutes.

3  Transfer chicken to carving board, tent with foil, and let rest for 20 minutes. Meanwhile, strain chicken juices from pot through fine-mesh strainer into fat separator, pressing on solids to extract liquid; discard solids. Let juices settle for 5 minutes, then pour into small saucepan and set over low heat. Carve chicken, adding any accumulated juices to saucepan. Season jus with lemon juice to taste. Serve chicken, passing jus separately.

# weeknight roast chicken

serves 3 to 4

“

My husband and I know this recipe by heart as it's our go-to method for roasting a whole chicken. It's just so easy and foolproof. Plus, I love telling the backstory of how this recipe was developed in the test kitchen. It all started when the power went out one day, wrecking a number of recipe tests as the ovens went down. A few half-cooked chickens were in some of the ovens and although the test was ruined, the test cook left the chickens in the still warm but off ovens to finish cooking so that the food didn't go to waste. Bingo: The best method for roast chicken was born. I will warn you that the skin doesn't get supercrisp on this roast chicken (which I don't really care much about), but the drippings left behind in the pan are the best and the fat has already risen to the top for easy skimming. ”

*julia*

1 (3½- to 4-pound) whole chicken, giblets discarded

1 tablespoon vegetable oil

Salt and pepper

1  Adjust oven rack to middle position, place 12-inch ovensafe skillet on rack, and heat oven to 450 degrees. Pat chicken dry with paper towels. Rub entire surface with oil, season with salt and pepper, and rub in with your hands to coat evenly. Tie legs together with twine and tuck wingtips behind back.

2  Transfer chicken, breast side up, to hot skillet in oven. Roast chicken until breast registers 120 degrees and thighs register 135 degrees, 25 to 35 minutes. Turn oven off and leave chicken in oven until breast registers 160 degrees and thighs register 175 degrees, 25 to 35 minutes.

3  Transfer chicken to carving board and let rest for 20 minutes. Carve and serve.

# pressure-cooker chicken noodle soup

serves 8

1 tablespoon vegetable oil

1 onion, chopped fine

3 garlic cloves, minced

1 teaspoon minced fresh thyme or ¼ teaspoon dried

8 cups water

4 carrots, peeled and sliced ½ inch thick

2 celery ribs, sliced ½ inch thick

2 tablespoons soy sauce

1 (4-pound) whole chicken, giblets discarded

Salt and pepper

4 ounces (2⅔ cups) wide egg noodles

¼ cup minced fresh parsley

"

Ian and I make chicken noodle soup all year long—it's our number one comfort food. Ian has his own recipe (and it's delicious) but I prefer to use the pressure cooker because it's easy, it's fast, and the flavor of the broth has an intense but clean chicken flavor. I grew up around pressure cookers and I still remember that metronome-like beat that the indicator made as it rocked back and forth with puffs of steam. Those old-school pots were fun to watch but my mother and I love the newer, sleeker versions (stovetop, not electric) with their easy-to-read indicators and straightforward quick-release valves. I always use organic chicken when making this soup because I think it has a better flavor. "

*julia*

1 Heat oil in pressure-cooker pot over medium heat until shimmering. Add onion and cook until softened, about 5 minutes. Stir in garlic and thyme and cook until fragrant, about 30 seconds. Stir in water, carrots, celery, and soy sauce, scraping up any browned bits. Season chicken with salt and pepper and place breast side up in pot.

2 Lock pressure cooker lid in place and bring to high pressure over medium-high heat. As soon as pot reaches high pressure, reduce heat to medium-low and cook for 20 minutes, adjusting heat as needed to maintain high pressure.

3 Remove pot from heat. Quick-release pressure, then carefully remove lid, allowing steam to escape away from you.

4 Transfer chicken to carving board and let cool slightly. Using 2 forks, shred chicken into bite-size pieces, discarding skin and bones. Meanwhile, using large spoon, skim excess fat from surface of soup. Bring soup to boil, stir in noodles, and cook until tender, about 5 minutes. Stir in shredded chicken and parsley, season with salt and pepper to taste, and serve.

### variation
### pressure-cooker chicken and rice soup

Substitute 1 cup long-grain white rice for egg noodles and cook until tender, 15 to 18 minutes, then continue as directed.

# chicken tikka masala

serves 4 to 6

6 tablespoons vegetable oil

1 onion, chopped fine

1 tablespoon garam masala

1 tablespoon grated fresh ginger

2 garlic cloves, minced

1 (28-ounce) can crushed tomatoes

⅔ cup heavy cream

1 cup plain Greek yogurt

Salt

1 teaspoon ground cumin

1 teaspoon ground coriander

½ teaspoon cayenne pepper

2 pounds boneless, skinless chicken breasts, trimmed

¼ cup minced fresh cilantro

"

Back in the early '90s, I traveled to the U.K. to meet my Scottish boyfriend's parents, who live outside of Glasgow. I was prepared to eat lots of fish and chips, but I fell in love with the amazing array of Indian and Pakistani restaurants. Before that trip, I'd had little exposure to Indian cuisine, but I ended up ordering "a curry" for lunch or dinner as many times as I could. A sweat-inducing vindaloo was my initial favorite, but I learned to love the creamy, soft flavors of tikka masala sauce. Turns out, chicken tikka masala was named a British national dish in 2001—seven years after I married my Scottish boyfriend. "

*bridget*

1 Combine oil and onion in Dutch oven and cook over medium-high heat until softened, about 5 minutes. Stir in garam masala, ginger, and garlic and cook until fragrant, about 30 seconds. Stir in tomatoes, cover, and simmer gently, stirring occasionally, until flavors meld, about 15 minutes. Stir in cream, cover, and keep warm.

2 Meanwhile, adjust oven rack 6 inches from broiler element and heat broiler. Line broiler-pan bottom with aluminum foil and lay slotted broiler pan on top. Combine yogurt, 1 teaspoon salt, cumin, coriander, and cayenne in medium bowl. Pound thicker ends of breasts as needed, then pat dry with paper towels.

3 Using tongs, dip chicken into yogurt mixture (chicken should be coated with thick layer of yogurt) and arrange on prepared broiler-pan top. Discard excess yogurt mixture. Broil chicken until lightly charred in spots and chicken registers 160 degrees, 10 to 18 minutes, flipping halfway through cooking.

4 Transfer chicken to cutting board, let rest for 5 minutes, then cut into 1-inch chunks. Stir chicken into warm sauce and let heat through, about 2 minutes. Stir in cilantro and season with salt to taste. Serve.

# chicken vindaloo

serves 6

3 pounds boneless, skinless chicken thighs, trimmed and cut into 1½-inch pieces

Salt and pepper

3 tablespoons vegetable oil

3 onions, chopped fine

8 garlic cloves, minced

1 tablespoon paprika

¾ teaspoon ground cumin

½ teaspoon ground cardamom

¼ teaspoon cayenne pepper

¼ teaspoon ground cloves

3 tablespoons all-purpose flour

1½ cups chicken broth

1 (14.5-ounce) can diced tomatoes

2 tablespoons red wine vinegar

1 tablespoon mustard seeds

2 bay leaves

1 teaspoon sugar

¼ cup minced fresh cilantro

1  Adjust oven rack to lower-middle position and heat oven to 325 degrees. Pat chicken dry with paper towels and season with salt and pepper. Heat 1 tablespoon oil in Dutch oven over medium-high heat until just smoking. Add half of chicken and brown well, about 8 minutes; transfer to bowl. Repeat with 1 tablespoon oil and remaining chicken.

2  Add remaining 1 tablespoon oil to now-empty pot and place over medium heat until shimmering. Add onions and ¼ teaspoon salt and cook until softened, 5 to 7 minutes. Stir in garlic, paprika, cumin, cardamom, cayenne, and cloves and cook until fragrant, about 30 seconds. Stir in flour and cook for 1 minute.

3  Gradually whisk in broth, scraping up any browned bits and smoothing out any lumps. Stir in tomatoes and their juice, vinegar, mustard seeds, bay leaves, sugar, and browned chicken with any accumulated juice. Bring to simmer. Cover pot, place in oven, and cook until chicken is tender, about 1 hour.

4  Remove stew from oven and remove bay leaves. Stir in cilantro, season with salt and pepper to taste, and serve.

# chicken enchiladas with red chile sauce

serves 4

¼ cup vegetable oil

1 onion, chopped fine

3 garlic cloves, minced

3 tablespoons chili powder

2 teaspoons ground coriander

2 teaspoons ground cumin

2 teaspoons sugar

½ teaspoon salt

1 pound boneless, skinless chicken thighs, trimmed and cut into ¼-inch-wide strips

2 (8-ounce) cans tomato sauce

1 cup water

½ cup minced fresh cilantro

¼ cup jarred jalapeños, chopped

12 ounces sharp cheddar cheese, shredded (3 cups)

12 (6-inch) corn tortillas

" Like most cooks, I appreciate a good 'cheater' ingredient. You know, something that shaves a little time or effort off of a recipe without a resulting drop in the quality or flavor of the final dish. Instead of toasting and simmering fresh or dried chiles for these enchiladas, good old chili powder, along with some ground coriander and cumin, is bloomed in hot oil to deepen its flavor. The other 'cheater' ingredient is pickled jalapeños, which add both spice and tang. And be sure to save some of that pickled jalapeño brine—it makes a mean 'spicy' martini. "

*bridget*

1  Heat 2 tablespoons oil in medium saucepan over medium-high heat until shimmering. Add onion and cook until softened, 5 to 7 minutes. Stir in garlic, chili powder, coriander, cumin, sugar, and salt and cook until fragrant, about 30 seconds. Stir in chicken and coat thoroughly with spices. Stir in tomato sauce and water, bring to simmer, and cook until chicken is cooked through, about 8 minutes.

2  Strain mixture through fine-mesh strainer into bowl, pressing on chicken and onion to extract as much sauce as possible; set sauce aside. Transfer chicken mixture to bowl, refrigerate for 20 minutes to chill, then stir in cilantro, jalapeños, and 2½ cups cheese.

3  Adjust oven rack to middle position and heat oven to 450 degrees. Spread ¾ cup sauce over bottom of 13 by 9-inch baking dish. Brush both sides of tortillas with remaining 2 tablespoons oil. Stack tortillas, wrap in damp dish towel, and place on plate; microwave until warm and pliable, about 1 minute.

4  Working with 1 warm tortilla at a time, spread ⅓ cup chicken filling across center of tortilla. Roll tortilla tightly around filling and place seam side down in baking dish; arrange enchiladas in 2 columns across width of dish.

5  Pour remaining sauce over top to cover completely and sprinkle with remaining ½ cup cheese. Cover dish tightly with greased aluminum foil and bake until enchiladas are heated through and cheese is melted, 15 to 20 minutes. Serve.

# classic ground beef tacos with homemade taco shells

serves 4

> Taco Tuesday is an actual thing at our house and this is the recipe we use. There's nothing unusual about it but it nails the combination of spices and the duo of canned tomato sauce and chicken broth for the sauce is brilliant. Marta doesn't like spicy food so we usually leave out the cayenne and pull out a selection of hot sauces for serving instead. Also, I always make a fresh cherry tomato relish to go alongside the tacos. On special occasions or for company (yes, I make this for casual company sometimes), I'll pull out all the stops and make homemade taco shells–they're out of this world. Just serve with all your favorite taco toppings. **"**

*julia*

1 tablespoon vegetable oil

1 onion, chopped fine

2 tablespoons chili powder

3 garlic cloves, minced

1 teaspoon ground cumin

1 teaspoon ground coriander

½ teaspoon dried oregano

¼ teaspoon cayenne pepper

Salt

1 pound 90 percent lean ground beef

½ cup canned tomato sauce

½ cup chicken broth

2 teaspoons cider vinegar

1 teaspoon packed light brown sugar

8 taco shells, warmed

1  Heat oil in 10-inch skillet over medium heat until shimmering. Add onion and cook until softened, about 5 minutes. Stir in chili powder, garlic, cumin, coriander, oregano, cayenne, and 1 teaspoon salt and cook until fragrant, about 30 seconds.

2  Stir in ground beef and cook, breaking up meat with wooden spoon, until no longer pink, about 5 minutes. Stir in tomato sauce, broth, vinegar, and sugar and simmer until thickened, about 10 minutes. Season with salt to taste. Divide filling evenly among taco shells and serve.

## homemade taco shells
makes 8

¾ cup vegetable oil

8 corn tortillas

1  In 8-inch skillet, heat vegetable oil to 350 degrees. Using tongs, slip half of tortilla into hot oil and submerge using metal spatula. Fry until just set, but not brown, about 30 seconds.

2  Flip tortilla. Hold tortilla open about 2 inches while keeping bottom submerged in oil. Fry until golden brown, about 1 ½ minutes. Flip again and fry other side until golden brown.

3  Transfer shell, upside down, to paper towel–lined baking sheet to drain. Repeat with remaining tortillas, keeping oil between 350 and 375 degrees.

## cherry tomato relish
makes 1½ cups

6 ounces grape tomatoes, quartered

3 scallions, sliced thin

2 tablespoons minced fresh cilantro

1 tablespoon extra-virgin olive oil

1 tablespoon lime juice

Salt and pepper

Combine all ingredients in bowl and season with salt and pepper to taste.

# pan-seared thick-cut steaks

serves 4

2 (1-pound) boneless strip steaks, 1½ to 1¾ inches thick, trimmed

Salt and pepper

1 tablespoon vegetable oil

1  Adjust oven rack to middle position and heat oven to 275 degrees. Pat steaks dry with paper towels. Cut each steak in half vertically to create four 8-ounce steaks. Season steaks with salt and pepper; gently press sides of steaks until uniform 1½ inches thick. Place steaks on wire rack set in rimmed baking sheet. Cook until meat registers 90 to 95 degrees (for rare to medium-rare), 20 to 25 minutes, or 100 to 105 degrees (for medium), 25 to 30 minutes.

2  Heat oil in 12-inch skillet over high heat until just smoking. Place steaks in skillet and sear until well browned and crusty, 1½ to 2 minutes, lifting once halfway through cooking to redistribute fat underneath each steak. (Reduce heat if fond begins to burn.) Using tongs, turn steaks and cook until well browned on second side, 2 to 2½ minutes. Transfer all steaks to clean wire rack and reduce heat under pan to medium. Use tongs to stand 2 steaks on their edges. Holding steaks together, return to skillet and sear on all sides until browned, about 1½ minutes. Repeat with remaining 2 steaks.

3  Transfer steaks to wire rack and let rest, tented with aluminum foil, for 10 minutes. Arrange steaks on individual plates and serve.

# easy grilled flank steak with garlic-herb sauce

serves 4 to 6

1 (2-pound) flank steak, trimmed

1 teaspoon sugar

Salt and pepper

1 cup minced fresh parsley

⅓ cup extra-virgin olive oil

2 tablespoons lemon juice

3 garlic cloves, minced

"
I absolutely love flank steak. I love it as much as, if not more than, any other fancy, expensive, dry-aged steak out there. I like its hearty flavor, its good chew, and its inexpensive price tag. We grill it for dinner at least once a week during the summer. There are only two keys to cooking flank steak: (1) don't overcook it and (2) slice it thin against the grain when serving. Also, this garlic-herb sauce is one of my all-time favorites and I often make similar sauces using whatever herbs are around. This sauce will make anything taste good, from steak, chicken, and fish to eggs, quinoa, and even tempeh. If you only have one sauce in your repertoire, it should be this one. "

*julia*

1 Pat steak dry with paper towels, sprinkle with ¾ teaspoon sugar, and season with salt and pepper. Combine parsley, oil, lemon juice, garlic, remaining ¼ teaspoon sugar, ¼ teaspoon salt, and ¼ teaspoon pepper in small bowl and set aside for serving.

2A For a charcoal grill Open bottom vent completely. Light large chimney starter filled with charcoal briquettes (6 quarts). When top coals are partially covered with ash, pour evenly over half of grill. Set cooking grate in place, cover, and open lid vent completely. Heat grill until hot, about 5 minutes.

2B For a gas grill Turn all burners to high, cover, and heat grill until hot, about 15 minutes. Leave primary burner on high and turn other burner(s) to medium.

3 Clean and oil cooking grate. Place steak on hotter side of grill. Cook (covered if using gas), turning as needed, until lightly charred and meat registers 120 to 125 degrees (for medium-rare), 8 to 12 minutes.

4 Transfer steak to carving board, tent with aluminum foil, and let rest for 5 to 10 minutes. Slice steak against grain very thin on bias and serve with garlic-herb sauce.

# flank steak in adobo

serves 4 to 6

### adobo

1½ ounces dried ancho chiles, stemmed and seeded

1 ounce dried pasilla chiles, stemmed and seeded

¾ cup salsa verde

¾ cup chicken broth

½ cup orange juice

⅓ cup packed brown sugar

¼ cup lime juice (2 limes)

1½ teaspoons dried oregano

1 teaspoon salt

½ teaspoon pepper

### flank steak

2½–3 pounds flank steak, trimmed and cut into 1½-inch cubes

Salt and pepper

2 tablespoons vegetable oil

1 onion, chopped fine

8 garlic cloves, minced

1 tablespoon ground cumin

12 (8-inch) flour tortillas, warmed

4 ounces queso fresco or mild feta, crumbled (1 cup)

½ cup coarsely chopped fresh cilantro

**1 For the adobo** Adjust oven rack to lower-middle position and heat oven to 350 degrees. Arrange anchos and pasillas on rimmed baking sheet and bake until fragrant, about 5 minutes. Immediately transfer chiles to bowl and cover with hot tap water. Let stand until chiles are softened and pliable, about 5 minutes. Drain.

**2** Process salsa verde, broth, orange juice, sugar, lime juice, oregano, salt, pepper, and drained chiles in blender until smooth, 1 to 2 minutes. Set aside.

**3 For the flank steak** Reduce oven temperature to 300 degrees. Pat beef dry with paper towels and sprinkle with ½ teaspoon salt and ½ teaspoon pepper. Heat 1 tablespoon oil in Dutch oven over medium-high heat until just smoking. Add half of beef and cook, stirring occasionally, until well browned on all sides, 6 to 9 minutes. (Adjust heat, if necessary, to keep bottom of pot from scorching.) Using slotted spoon, transfer beef to large bowl. Repeat with remaining 1 tablespoon oil and remaining beef.

**4** Add onion and ½ teaspoon salt to now-empty pot. Reduce heat to medium and cook, stirring occasionally, until golden brown, 3 to 5 minutes, scraping up any browned bits. Add garlic and cumin and cook until fragrant, about 30 seconds. Stir in adobo, beef, and any accumulated juices until well incorporated and bring mixture to simmer.

**5** Cover pot and transfer to oven. Cook until beef is tender and sauce has thickened, about 1½ hours. Season with salt and pepper to taste. Serve with flour tortillas, sprinkled with queso fresco and cilantro.

# hearty beef and vegetable stew

serves 4 to 6

> Beef stew was a common winter dinner when I was growing up and my mother always threw in a few extra vegetables beyond the basic potatoes and carrots. This recipe reminds me of my mother's stew, with all the vegetables including portobello mushrooms, parsnips, and kale. I like this version not only because it's healthier, but also because the extra vegetables lend their own clean, fresh flavors to the gravy. This is another recipe that I often scale up so that some can go into the freezer for an easy meal down the road. I know that using two types of broth (chicken and beef) seems a little fussy but I do like the neutral flavor they have when combined. For wine, I usually use a Pinot Noir because it's my favorite to drink.

*julia*

2 pounds boneless beef chuck-eye roast, trimmed and cut into 1½-inch pieces

Salt and pepper

5 teaspoons canola oil

1 large portobello mushroom cap, cut into ½-inch pieces

2 onions, chopped fine

3 garlic cloves, minced

1 tablespoon minced fresh thyme or 1 teaspoon dried

3 tablespoons all-purpose flour

1 tablespoon tomato paste

1½ cups dry red wine

2 cups chicken broth

2 cups beef broth

2 bay leaves

12 ounces red potatoes, unpeeled, cut into 1-inch pieces

4 carrots, peeled, halved lengthwise, and sliced 1 inch thick

4 parsnips, peeled, halved lengthwise, and sliced 1 inch thick

1 pound kale, stemmed and sliced into ½-inch-wide strips

½ cup frozen peas

¼ cup minced fresh parsley

1 Adjust oven rack to lower-middle position and heat oven to 300 degrees. Pat beef dry with paper towels and season with salt and pepper. Heat 1 teaspoon oil in Dutch oven over medium-high heat until just smoking. Brown half of meat on all sides, 5 to 10 minutes; transfer to bowl. Repeat with 1 teaspoon oil and remaining beef; transfer to bowl.

2 Add mushroom pieces to fat left in pot, cover, and cook over medium heat until softened and wet, about 5 minutes. Uncover and continue to cook until mushroom pieces are dry and browned, 5 to 10 minutes.

3 Stir in remaining 1 tablespoon oil and onions and cook until softened, 5 to 7 minutes. Stir in garlic and thyme and cook until fragrant, about 30 seconds. Stir in flour and tomato paste and cook until flour is lightly browned, about 1 minute.

4 Slowly whisk in wine, scraping up any browned bits. Slowly whisk in chicken broth and beef broth until smooth. Stir in bay leaves and browned meat and bring to simmer. Cover, transfer pot to oven, and cook for 1½ hours.

5 Stir in potatoes, carrots, and parsnips and continue to cook in oven until meat and vegetables are tender, about 1 hour. Stir in kale and continue to cook in oven until tender, about 10 minutes. Remove stew from oven and remove bay leaves. Stir in peas and parsley and let stew sit for 5 to 10 minutes. Season with salt and pepper to taste. Serve.

# bacon-wrapped pork loin with roasted red potatoes

serves 4 to 6

12 ounces bacon

1 (2½- to 3-pound) boneless pork loin roast, trimmed

2 teaspoons ground fennel

Salt and pepper

2½ pounds small red potatoes, unpeeled, halved

3 tablespoons vegetable oil

"

I remember the first time I made this recipe at home for Ian. He went nuts for it! I also remember that after dinner, Ian and I kept going back for just one more potato as we cleaned up the dishes. The pork is delicious with the ground fennel seed and bacon, but the potatoes are perfection, with beautifully roasted bottoms and just a hint of bacon flavor. The hardest thing about this recipe, for me, is tracking down a good pork loin. I'm fussy about pork and hate the flavor of enhanced pork, so I usually have to make a special trip to a high-end grocery store or order one through the butcher here at work. I love serving this dish with braised red cabbage or roasted Brussels sprouts. "

*julia*

1 Adjust oven rack to upper-middle position and heat oven to 375 degrees. Lay bacon strips on large plate and weigh down with second plate. Microwave until slightly shriveled but still pliable, 1 to 3 minutes. Transfer bacon to paper towel–lined plate and let cool slightly.

2 Line rimmed baking sheet with aluminum foil. Pat pork dry with paper towels, rub with fennel, and season with salt and pepper. Place pork in center of prepared baking sheet. Lay bacon attractively over top of pork, slightly overlapping slices and tucking ends underneath roast.

3 Toss potatoes with 2 tablespoons oil in bowl and season with salt and pepper. Brush baking sheet around pork loin with remaining 1 tablespoon oil. Lay potatoes, cut side down, on oiled baking sheet around pork. Roast pork and potatoes until pork registers 130 degrees, 40 minutes to 1 hour, rotating baking sheet halfway through roasting.

4 Remove pork and potatoes from oven, position oven rack 6 inches from broiler element, and heat broiler. Broil pork and potatoes until bacon is crisp and browned and pork registers 140 degrees, 3 to 5 minutes.

5 Transfer pork to carving board and let rest for 15 to 20 minutes. Turn oven off and return potatoes to warm oven until serving time. Cut pork into ½-inch-thick slices and serve with potatoes.

# crispy cornflake pork chops

serves 4

1½ cups (1½ ounces) cornflakes

½ cup cornstarch

Salt and pepper

½ cup buttermilk

1 tablespoon Dijon mustard

1 garlic clove, minced

4 (3- to 4-ounce) boneless pork chops, ½ to ¾ inch thick, trimmed

⅓ cup vegetable oil

Lemon wedges

"Ian's nickname is Pork Chop because it's his all-time favorite food. So it's not surprising that we eat a lot of chops at our house. This cornflake-crusted version is a family favorite. I love the sweet flavor and supercrunchy texture of the cornflakes with the pork. And thanks to the cornstarch in the breading and the crosshatching method on the chops, the cornflake coating stays put during cooking. Once, Ian bought cornflake crumbs to try and streamline the recipe prep, but they didn't taste nearly as good (very stale) so avoid them. And if you don't have buttermilk on hand (I rarely do), you can substitute 6 tablespoons of plain yogurt mixed with 2 tablespoons of milk. Ian and Marta like to eat these chops with applesauce, but I prefer a squeeze of fresh lemon juice."

*julia*

1  Process cornflakes, 3 tablespoons cornstarch, ½ teaspoon salt, and ½ teaspoon pepper in food processor until cornflakes are finely ground, about 10 seconds; transfer to shallow dish. Spread remaining 5 tablespoons cornstarch in second shallow dish. Whisk buttermilk, mustard, and garlic together in third shallow dish.

2  Using sharp knife, cut ½-inch-wide crosshatch pattern on both sides of each chop, about ¹⁄₁₆ inch deep. Season chops with salt and pepper. Working with 1 chop at a time, dredge in cornstarch, then dip in buttermilk mixture, and finally coat with cornflake mixture, pressing gently to adhere. Transfer chops to wire rack set in rimmed baking sheet.

3  Heat oil in 12-inch nonstick skillet over medium-high heat until shimmering. Add chops and cook until golden and crisp on both sides and center of chops registers 140 degrees, 4 to 10 minutes, flipping halfway through cooking. Let chops drain briefly on paper towel–lined plate before serving with lemon wedges.

# fish meunière with browned butter and lemon

serves 4 to 6

### fish

½ cup all-purpose flour

4 (5- to 6-ounce) skinless sole or flounder fillets, ⅜ inch thick

Salt and pepper

2 tablespoons vegetable oil

2 tablespoons unsalted butter, cut into 2 pieces

### browned butter

4 tablespoons unsalted butter, cut into 4 pieces

1 tablespoon chopped fresh parsley

1½ tablespoons lemon juice, plus lemon wedges for serving

Salt

1  **For the fish**  Adjust oven rack to lower-middle position and heat oven to 200 degrees. Set 4 plates on rack. Spread flour in shallow dish. Pat fillets dry with paper towels, season both sides generously with salt and pepper, and let stand until fillets are glistening with moisture, about 5 minutes. Coat both sides of fillets with flour, shake off excess, and place in single layer on baking sheet.

2  Heat 1 tablespoon oil in 12-inch nonstick skillet over high heat until shimmering, then add 1 tablespoon butter and swirl to coat pan bottom. Carefully place 2 fillets, skinned side up, in skillet. Immediately reduce heat to medium-high and cook, without moving fish, until edges of fillets are opaque and bottom is golden brown, about 3 minutes. Using 2 spatulas, gently flip fillets and cook until fish flakes apart when gently prodded with paring knife, about 2 minutes longer. Carefully transfer each fillet to warmed plate, keeping skinned side down, and return plates to oven. Wipe out skillet with paper towels and repeat with remaining 1 tablespoon oil, remaining 1 tablespoon butter, and remaining 2 fillets.

3  **For the browned butter**  Heat butter in 10-inch skillet over medium-high heat until butter melts, 1 to 1½ minutes. Continue to cook, swirling pan constantly, until butter is golden brown and has nutty aroma, 1 to 1½ minutes. Remove skillet from heat.

4  Remove plates from oven and sprinkle fillets with parsley. Add lemon juice to browned butter and season with salt to taste. Spoon sauce over fillets and serve immediately with lemon wedges.

# lemon-herb cod fillets with crispy garlic potatoes

serves 4

1½ pounds russet potatoes, unpeeled, sliced into ¼-inch-thick rounds

2 tablespoons unsalted butter, melted, plus 3 tablespoons cut into ¼-inch pieces

3 garlic cloves, minced

4 sprigs fresh thyme, plus 1 teaspoon minced

Salt and pepper

4 (6- to 8-ounce) skinless cod fillets, 1 to 1½ inches thick

1 lemon, sliced thin

"

This cod and potato recipe is so easy that it feels like cheating, like I'm not really cooking. The potatoes get wonderfully browned and crisp around the edges and the cod always turns out perfectly done. Cooking the fish and potatoes together also allows their flavors to mingle in a nice way and makes cleanup a breeze. Not to mention, this dish is a looker, with the thyme sprigs and slices of lemon on top of the fish. It's a great option for a casual dinner with friends. I love cod, but haddock or halibut could be substituted for the cod if you like. I serve this with a simple side salad for an easy, healthy, no-fuss meal. "

*julia*

1  Adjust oven rack to lower-middle position and heat oven to 425 degrees. Toss potatoes, melted butter, garlic, minced thyme, ½ teaspoon salt, and ¼ teaspoon pepper together in bowl.

2  Shingle potatoes into four 6 by 4-inch rectangular piles on parchment paper–lined rimmed baking sheet. Roast potatoes until spotty brown and just tender, 30 to 35 minutes, rotating sheet halfway through roasting.

3  Pat cod dry with paper towels and season with salt and pepper. Lay 1 cod fillet skinned side down on top of each potato pile and top evenly with butter pieces, thyme sprigs, and lemon slices. Bake until cod flakes apart when gently prodded with paring knife and registers 140 degrees, about 15 minutes.

4  To serve, slide spatula underneath potatoes and cod and gently transfer to individual plates.

# shrimp and grits

serves 4

> Before my husband and I moved to Boston, we ventured to Charleston, South Carolina, to see what the restaurant job market was like (he is also a chef). I'll never forget how the Charleston folks went out of their way to make us feel welcome. In each restaurant we visited, the chef would take time to make us a meal to enjoy during our chat. One older chef–transplanted from Paris 40 years prior–prepared such a simple but elegant lunch of shrimp and grits. The shrimp–just pulled in from a trawler–were still head-on, and so succulent. The grits-creamy and tender-were poured hot out of the saucepan. It was this singular dish that taught me that simple cooking can also be fine dining, if the ingredients are left to shine.
>
> *bridget*

### grits

3 tablespoons unsalted butter

1 cup grits

2¼ cups whole milk

2 cups water

Salt and pepper

### shrimp

3 tablespoons unsalted butter

1½ pounds extra-large shrimp (21 to 25 per pound), peeled and deveined, shells reserved

1 tablespoon tomato paste

2¼ cups water

3 slices bacon, cut into ½-inch pieces

1 garlic clove, minced

Salt and pepper

2 tablespoons all-purpose flour

1 tablespoon lemon juice

½ teaspoon hot sauce, plus extra for serving

4 scallions, sliced thin

**1** **For the grits** Melt 1 tablespoon butter in medium saucepan over medium heat. Add grits and cook, stirring often, until fragrant, about 3 minutes. Add milk, water, and ¾ teaspoon salt. Increase heat to medium-high and bring to boil. Reduce heat to low, cover, and simmer, whisking often, until thick and creamy, about 25 minutes. Remove from heat, stir in remaining 2 tablespoons butter, and season with salt and pepper to taste. Cover and keep warm.

**2** **For the shrimp** Meanwhile, melt 1 tablespoon butter in 12-inch nonstick skillet over medium heat. Add shrimp shells and cook, stirring occasionally, until shells are spotty brown, about 7 minutes. Stir in tomato paste and cook for 30 seconds. Add water and bring to boil. Reduce heat to low, cover, and simmer for 5 minutes.

**3** Strain shrimp stock through fine-mesh strainer set over bowl, pressing on solids to extract as much liquid as possible; discard solids. You should have about 1 ½ cups stock (add more water if necessary to equal 1 ½ cups). Wipe out skillet with paper towels.

**4** Cook bacon in skillet over medium-low heat until crisp, 7 to 9 minutes. Increase heat to medium-high and stir in shrimp, garlic, ½ teaspoon salt, and ½ teaspoon pepper. Cook until edges of shrimp are just beginning to turn pink, but shrimp are not cooked through, about 2 minutes. Transfer shrimp mixture to bowl.

**5** Melt 1 tablespoon butter in now-empty skillet over medium-high heat. Whisk in flour and cook for 1 minute. Slowly whisk in shrimp stock until incorporated. Bring to boil, reduce heat to medium-low, and simmer until thickened slightly, about 5 minutes.

**6** Stir in shrimp mixture, cover, and cook until shrimp are cooked through, about 3 minutes. Off heat, stir in lemon juice, hot sauce, and remaining 1 tablespoon butter. Season with salt and pepper to taste. Serve over grits, sprinkled with scallions, and passing extra hot sauce separately.

# grilled swordfish and lime skewers

serves 4

1 large red onion, cut into 1-inch pieces, 3 layers thick

5 tablespoons extra-virgin olive oil

1 tablespoon ground coriander

1 teaspoon ground cumin

1 teaspoon sugar

Salt and pepper

1 (1½-pound) skinless swordfish steak, cut into 1¼-inch pieces

3 limes, halved, then each half quartered

2 tablespoons chopped fresh cilantro

1½ teaspoons minced shallot

"Truth be told, Ian is usually the one who cooks this at our house; he always nails the doneness of the swordfish so that it's cooked all the way through but isn't dry. The best part of this recipe, however, is the juice from the grilled limes. Grilling the limes deepens their flavor and makes them taste sweeter. The combination of the cilantro-shallot oil and juice from the limes drizzled over the grilled fish is a winner. When my family is on vacation in the Keys, we often swap mahi-mahi for the swordfish. Also, I bought Ian some double-pronged, seafood-themed skewers for Father's Day a few years back and I think they work better than single-pronged skewers for this recipe."

*julia*

1 Gently toss onion with 1 tablespoon oil in bowl, cover, and microwave until just tender, about 2 minutes. Combine 2 tablespoons oil, coriander, cumin, sugar, ½ teaspoon salt, and ½ teaspoon pepper in large bowl. Pat fish dry with paper towels, add to spice mixture, and toss gently to coat. Thread fish, limes, and onion evenly onto four 12-inch metal skewers, in alternating pattern.

2A For a charcoal grill Open bottom vent completely. Light large chimney starter filled with charcoal briquettes (6 quarts). When top coals are partially covered with ash, pour evenly over grill. Set cooking grate in place, cover, and open lid vent completely. Heat grill until hot, about 5 minutes.

2B For a gas grill Turn all burners to high, cover, and heat grill until hot, about 15 minutes. Turn all burners to medium-high.

3 Clean cooking grate, then repeatedly brush grate with well-oiled paper towels until black and glossy, 5 to 10 times. Place skewers on grill. Cook (covered if using gas), turning as needed, until fish is opaque and flakes apart when gently prodded with paring knife, 5 to 8 minutes.

4 Transfer skewers to platter, tent with aluminum foil, and let rest for 5 minutes. Combine remaining 2 tablespoons oil, cilantro, and shallot in bowl and season with salt and pepper to taste. Brush skewers with oil mixture before serving.

# spaghetti with lemon, basil, and scallops

serves 4 to 6

½ cup extra-virgin olive oil

2 teaspoons grated lemon zest plus ⅓ cup juice (2 lemons)

1 small garlic clove, minced to paste

Salt and pepper

2 ounces Parmesan cheese, grated (1 cup)

4 tablespoons unsalted butter, softened

1 pound small bay scallops

1 pound spaghetti

¼ cup shredded fresh basil

"

Growing up, we ate a simple pasta dish with scallops much like this one. In fact, I served it for a group of high-school friends at my house before our junior prom. (I also remember splattering a little of the sauce on my prom dress.) There's just something about the simplicity and elegance of this dish that works. Rather than drowning the seafood in a heavy tomato sauce, this recipe brings out the scallops' flavor with a no-cook lemon vinaigrette and a handful of fresh basil. This dish works equally well as a last-minute supper or an easy dinner with friends. Because this recipe is so simple, it is important to use high-quality extra-virgin olive oil, freshly squeezed lemon juice, and fresh basil. "

*julia*

1 Whisk oil, lemon zest and juice, garlic, and ½ teaspoon salt together in small bowl, then stir in Parmesan until thick and creamy.

2 Melt 2 tablespoons butter in 12-inch nonstick skillet over medium heat. Pat scallops dry with paper towels and season with salt and pepper. Add scallops in single layer and cook until scallops are firm, about 3 minutes; transfer to bowl and cover.

3 Meanwhile, bring 4 quarts water to boil in large pot. Add pasta and 1 tablespoon salt and cook, stirring often, until al dente. Reserve ½ cup cooking water, then drain pasta and return it to pot. Stir in olive oil mixture, scallops with any accumulated juices, remaining 2 tablespoons butter, and basil and toss to combine. Add reserved cooking water as needed to adjust consistency and season with salt and pepper to taste. Serve.

# pasta with classic bolognese

serves 4 to 6

5 tablespoons unsalted butter

2 tablespoons finely chopped onion

2 tablespoons minced carrot

2 tablespoons minced celery

12 ounces meatloaf mix

Salt and pepper

1 cup whole milk

1 cup dry white wine

1 (28-ounce) can whole peeled tomatoes, drained with juice reserved, tomatoes chopped fine

1 pound fettuccine or linguine

Grated Parmesan cheese

1 Melt 3 tablespoons butter in Dutch oven over medium heat. Add onion, carrot, and celery and cook until softened, 5 to 7 minutes. Stir in meatloaf mix and ½ teaspoon salt and cook, breaking up meat with wooden spoon, until no longer pink, about 3 minutes.

2 Stir in milk, bring to simmer, and cook until milk evaporates and only rendered fat remains, 10 to 15 minutes. Stir in wine, bring to simmer, and cook until wine evaporates, 10 to 15 minutes.

3 Stir in tomatoes and reserved tomato juice and bring to simmer. Reduce heat to low so that sauce continues to simmer just barely, with occasional bubble or two at surface, until liquid has evaporated, about 3 hours. Season with salt to taste. (Sauce can be refrigerated for up to 2 days or frozen for up to 1 month.)

4 Meanwhile, bring 4 quarts water to boil in large pot. Add pasta and 1 tablespoon salt and cook, stirring often, until al dente. Reserve ½ cup cooking water, then drain pasta and return it to pot. Add sauce and remaining 2 tablespoons butter and toss to combine. Season with salt and pepper to taste and add reserved cooking water as needed to adjust consistency. Serve with Parmesan.

# beef ragu with warm spices

serves 4 to 6

1½ pounds boneless beef short ribs, trimmed

Salt and pepper

1 tablespoon olive oil

1 onion, chopped fine

2 tablespoons minced fresh parsley

½ teaspoon ground cinnamon

Pinch ground cloves

½ cup red wine

1 (28-ounce) can whole peeled tomatoes, drained with juice reserved, tomatoes chopped fine

1 pound rigatoni

Grated Parmesan cheese

"

I didn't fall in love with this recipe until I started working at ATK. In fact, I'd never had a meaty tomato sauce flavored with cinnamon and cloves before. The pairing of these flavors is magical, and I find myself using it in lots of ways besides tomato sauce (with steak, stews, and other beef braises). I often double this recipe and store a batch in the freezer for a rainy day. Be sure to trim as much fat as possible from the ribs or else the sauce may be greasy. "

*julia*

1  Pat ribs dry with paper towels and season with salt and pepper. Heat oil in 12-inch skillet over medium-high heat until just smoking. Brown ribs well on all sides, 8 to 10 minutes; transfer to plate.

2  Pour off all but 1 teaspoon fat left in skillet, add onion, and cook over medium heat until softened, about 5 minutes. Stir in parsley, cinnamon, and cloves and cook until fragrant, about 30 seconds. Stir in wine, scraping up any browned bits, and simmer until nearly evaporated, about 2 minutes.

3  Stir in tomatoes and reserved tomato juice. Nestle browned ribs into sauce, along with any accumulated juices, and bring to gentle simmer. Reduce heat to low, cover, and simmer gently, turning ribs occasionally, until meat is very tender and falling off bones, about 2 hours.

4  Transfer ribs to plate, let cool slightly, then shred meat into bite-size pieces, discarding fat and bones. Return shredded meat to sauce, bring to simmer, and cook until heated through and thickened slightly, about 5 minutes. Season with salt and pepper to taste.

5  Meanwhile, bring 4 quarts water to boil in large pot. Add pasta and 1 tablespoon salt and cook, stirring often, until al dente. Reserve ½ cup cooking water, then drain pasta and return it to pot. Add sauce and toss to combine. Season with salt and pepper to taste and add reserved cooking water as needed to adjust consistency. Serve with Parmesan.

# spaghetti alla carbonara

serves 4 to 6

¼ cup extra-virgin olive oil

8 slices bacon, cut into ¼-inch pieces

½ cup dry white wine

3 large eggs

1½ ounces Parmesan cheese, grated (¾ cup)

¼ cup finely grated Pecorino Romano cheese

2 garlic cloves, minced

1 pound spaghetti

Salt and pepper

"
I'm sometimes asked for ways to make certain dishes lighter, or healthier. While some are natural candidates for a healthy makeover, *spaghetti alla carbonara*, in my opinion, is not. Carbonara should be saved for those times when only a rich dish will do, and the fat in the recipe is not just there for fat's sake, it prevents the eggs in the dish from scrambling. My favorite way to enjoy spaghetti carbonara is as a first course. A small plate of it goes a long way, and a perfect second course is a plate of seared scallops and arugula salad. Pour yourself a glass of wine and live a little. "

*bridget*

1 Adjust oven rack to lower-middle position, set large ovensafe serving bowl on rack, and heat oven to 200 degrees.

2 Heat oil in 12-inch skillet over medium heat until shimmering. Add bacon and cook until crisp, about 8 minutes. Stir in wine, bring to simmer, and cook until slightly reduced, 6 to 8 minutes. Remove from heat and cover to keep warm. In separate bowl, whisk eggs, Parmesan, Pecorino, and garlic together.

3 Meanwhile, bring 4 quarts water to boil in large pot. Add pasta and 1 tablespoon salt and cook, stirring often, until al dente. Reserve ⅓ cup cooking water, then drain pasta and transfer to warmed serving bowl.

4 Immediately pour bacon mixture and egg mixture over hot pasta and toss to combine. Season with salt and pepper to taste and add reserved cooking water as needed to adjust consistency. Serve immediately.

# spaghetti with turkey-pesto meatballs

serves 4 to 6

1½ pounds 93 percent lean ground turkey

1 (7-ounce) container prepared basil pesto (⅔ cup)

⅔ cup panko bread crumbs

Salt and pepper

3 (14.5-ounce) cans diced tomatoes

1 tablespoon extra-virgin olive oil

1 onion, chopped fine

4 garlic cloves, minced

Pinch red pepper flakes

1 pound spaghetti

3 tablespoons chopped fresh basil

> At Chez Moi (Ian and Marta's name for our kitchen), meatballs are always the house special on Mondays. We've made lots of different meatballs at home over the years but this simple recipe is the one we use the most because it is so incredibly easy. We never eat all the meatballs in one sitting, so a few get packed into Marta's lunchbox for the following day and the rest go into the freezer or are eaten as 'snacks' over the next few days. Yup–no shame in a good meatball snack. Ian and I often swap ground beef and/or ground pork for the turkey depending on our mood. 99
>
> *julia*

1  Gently mix turkey, pesto, panko, ½ teaspoon salt, and ¼ teaspoon pepper in bowl using your hands until uniform. Shape mixture into eighteen 1½-inch meatballs.

2  Pulse 2 cans diced tomatoes and their juice in food processor until mostly smooth, about 12 pulses; set aside. Heat oil in 12-inch non-stick skillet over medium heat until just smoking. Brown meatballs well on all sides, about 10 minutes; transfer to paper towel–lined plate.

3  Add onion and ⅛ teaspoon salt to fat left in skillet and cook over medium heat until softened, 5 to 7 minutes. Stir in garlic and pepper flakes and cook until fragrant, about 30 seconds. Stir in processed tomatoes and remaining 1 can diced tomatoes and their juice. Bring to simmer and cook for 10 minutes. Return meatballs to skillet, cover, and simmer gently until meatballs are cooked through, about 10 minutes. (Sauce and meatballs can be refrigerated for up to 3 days or frozen for up to 1 month.)

4  Meanwhile, bring 4 quarts water to boil in large pot. Add pasta and 1 tablespoon salt and cook, stirring often, until al dente. Reserve 1 cup cooking water, then drain pasta and return it to pot. Add several large spoonfuls of tomato sauce (without meatballs) to pasta and toss to combine. Season with salt and pepper to taste and add reserved cooking water as needed to adjust consistency. Divide pasta among individual bowls. Top each bowl with remaining sauce and meatballs, sprinkle with basil, and serve.

# meatballs and marinara

serves 8

## onion mixture

¼ cup olive oil

3 onions, chopped fine

8 garlic cloves, minced

1 tablespoon dried oregano

¾ teaspoon red pepper flakes

## marinara

1 (6-ounce) can tomato paste

1 cup dry red wine

4 (28-ounce) cans crushed tomatoes

1 cup water

1 ounce Parmesan cheese, grated (½ cup)

¼ cup chopped fresh basil

Salt

Sugar

## meatballs

4 slices hearty white sandwich bread, torn into pieces

¾ cup milk

8 ounces sweet Italian sausage, casings removed

2 ounces Parmesan cheese, grated (1 cup)

½ cup chopped fresh parsley

2 large eggs

2 garlic cloves, minced

1½ teaspoons salt

2½ pounds 80 percent lean ground chuck

> This recipe is a home run! I love that a sautéed base of onions, garlic, and herbs flavors both the sauce and the meatballs. I love that the meatballs are BIG, and baked rather than fried. And I love that the sauce is hearty and rich without tasting overcooked. Seriously, this recipe never fails, and even the aroma from the sauce and meatballs was once enough to get our postman to knock on my front door and ask what I was cooking. (I packed a to-go container for him to take home.) This recipe makes enough to sauce 2 pounds of pasta.

*bridget*

1  For the onion mixture  Heat oil in Dutch oven over medium-high heat until shimmering. Add onions and cook until golden brown, 10 to 15 minutes. Add garlic, oregano, and pepper flakes and cook until fragrant, about 30 seconds. Transfer half of onion mixture to large bowl; set aside.

2  For the marinara  Add tomato paste to onion mixture remaining in pot and cook until fragrant, about 1 minute. Add wine and cook until slightly thickened, about 2 minutes. Stir in crushed tomatoes and water and simmer over low heat until sauce has thickened, 45 minutes to 1 hour. Stir in Parmesan and basil. Season with salt and sugar to taste.

3  For the meatballs  Meanwhile, adjust oven rack to upper-middle position and heat oven to 475 degrees. Using fork, mash bread and milk into reserved onion mixture in bowl until thoroughly combined. Add sausage, Parmesan, parsley, eggs, garlic, and salt and mash to combine. Add beef and gently knead with your hands until combined (do not overwork). Gently form mixture into sixteen 2½-inch meatballs, place on rimmed baking sheet, and bake until well browned, about 20 minutes.

4  Transfer meatballs to pot with sauce and simmer for 15 minutes. Serve.

*Cooking at Home with Bridget and Julia*

# skillet campanelle with fresh tomato sauce

serves 4

2 tablespoons extra-virgin olive oil

1 onion, chopped fine

4 garlic cloves, minced

1 tablespoon tomato paste

2 pounds tomatoes, cored and cut into ½-inch pieces

Salt and pepper

½ cup dry white wine

3½ cups water, plus extra as needed

12 ounces (3¾ cups) campanelle

¼ cup chopped fresh basil

Grated Parmesan cheese

**1** Heat oil in 12-inch nonstick skillet over medium heat until shimmering. Add onion and cook until softened, 5 to 7 minutes. Stir in garlic and tomato paste and cook until fragrant, about 1 minute. Stir in tomatoes, 1 teaspoon salt, and ½ teaspoon pepper and cook until tomato pieces lose their shape, 5 to 7 minutes. Stir in wine and simmer for 2 minutes.

**2** Stir in water and pasta. Cover, increase heat to medium-high, and cook at vigorous simmer, stirring often, until pasta is nearly tender, about 12 minutes.

**3** Uncover and continue to simmer, tossing pasta gently, until pasta is tender and sauce has thickened, 3 to 5 minutes; if sauce becomes too thick, add extra water as needed. Off heat, stir in basil and season with salt and pepper to taste. Serve with Parmesan.

“

This recipe reminds me of a meal I had in Tuscany before I went to culinary school. I was traveling with lots of family, and one night, a bunch of my cousins and I traveled into Florence for a night out. We ate dinner in a popular restaurant and while everyone ordered fairly fancy things, I ordered a simple plate of *pasta al pomodoro*. It was like nothing I'd ever eaten before. I could taste the wheat of the pasta, the sunshine on the tomatoes, and a hint of the rosemary breeze that followed us everywhere in Tuscany. It was an eye-opener that something so simple could taste so good. Now, this recipe isn't a replication of that meal by any stretch, but it gets closer than anything I've tasted since. I think it's because the pasta is simmered right in the sauce made of fresh tomatoes. Anyway, every time I make this I fondly remember my family trip to Italy. ”

*julia*

# pasta e ceci

serves 4 to 6

2 ounces pancetta, cut into ½-inch pieces

1 small carrot, peeled and cut into ½-inch pieces

1 small celery rib, cut into ½-inch pieces

4 garlic cloves, peeled

1 onion, halved and cut into 1-inch pieces

1 (14.5-ounce) can whole peeled tomatoes, drained

¼ cup extra-virgin olive oil, plus extra for serving

1 anchovy fillet, rinsed, patted dry, and minced

¼ teaspoon red pepper flakes

2 teaspoons minced fresh rosemary

2 (15-ounce) cans chickpeas (do not drain)

2 cups water

Salt and pepper

8 ounces (1½ cups) ditalini

1 tablespoon lemon juice

1 tablespoon minced fresh parsley

1 ounce Parmesan cheese, grated (½ cup)

1  Process pancetta in food processor until ground to paste, about 30 seconds, scraping down sides of bowl as needed. Add carrot, celery, and garlic and pulse until finely chopped, 8 to 10 pulses. Add onion and pulse until onion is cut into $\frac{1}{8}$- to $\frac{1}{4}$-inch pieces, 8 to 10 pulses. Transfer pancetta mixture to Dutch oven. Pulse tomatoes in now-empty food processor until coarsely chopped, 8 to 10 pulses. Set aside.

2  Add oil to pancetta mixture in Dutch oven and cook over medium heat, stirring frequently, until fond begins to form on bottom of pot, about 5 minutes. Add anchovy, pepper flakes, and rosemary and cook until fragrant, about 1 minute. Stir in tomatoes, chickpeas and their liquid, water, and 1 teaspoon salt and bring to boil, scraping up any browned bits. Reduce heat to medium-low and simmer for 10 minutes. Add pasta and cook, stirring frequently, until tender, 10 to 12 minutes. Stir in lemon juice and parsley and season with salt and pepper to taste. Serve, passing Parmesan and extra oil separately.

*Home-Style Dinners*

# pasta with kale and sunflower seed pesto

serves 4 to 6

2 unpeeled garlic cloves

4 ounces kale, stemmed and chopped (2 cups)

1 cup fresh basil leaves

1½ ounces Parmesan cheese, grated (¾ cup), plus extra for serving

½ cup raw sunflower seeds, toasted

1 teaspoon red pepper flakes (optional)

Salt and pepper

½ cup extra-virgin olive oil

1 pound fusilli

1  Toast garlic in 8-inch skillet over medium heat, stirring often, until fragrant, 5 to 7 minutes; transfer to bowl. Let garlic cool slightly, then peel and mince.

2  Pulse kale, basil, Parmesan, sunflower seeds, pepper flakes, if using, ½ teaspoon pepper, and garlic in food processor until finely ground, 20 to 30 pulses, scraping down bowl as needed. With processor running, slowly add oil until incorporated. Transfer to medium bowl and season with salt and pepper to taste.

3  Meanwhile, bring 4 quarts water to boil in large pot. Add pasta and 1 tablespoon salt and cook, stirring often, until al dente. Reserve ¾ cup cooking water, then drain pasta and return it to pot. Stir several tablespoons of reserved pasta water into pesto to loosen it, then add it to pasta and toss to combine. Adjust consistency with remaining reserved cooking water as needed and season with salt and pepper to taste. Serve with extra Parmesan.

“

My mother loves kale so we ate a lot of it growing up. In fact, her German father, my opa, used to grow an entire vegetable garden of nothing but kale and it was massive! When we visited him, the trunk of our white 1970 Dodge Dart would inevitably get filled with huge bunches of the stuff before we headed home. Luckily, kale wasn't a hard sell on me as a kid; I liked its soft but chewy texture in my mother's potato-sausage soup. Nowadays, kale is so hip that it has its own hashtag and lots of folks are finding neat, new ways to use it, as with this killer kale and sunflower seed pesto. I love the combination of basil and kale along with the assertive flavor of the sunflower seeds. ”

*julia*

# stovetop mac and cheese

serves 4

8 ounces (2 cups) elbow macaroni

Salt and pepper

2 large eggs

1 (12-ounce) can evaporated milk

1 teaspoon dry mustard dissolved in 1 teaspoon water

¼ teaspoon hot sauce

4 tablespoons unsalted butter

12 ounces cheddar cheese, shredded (3 cups)

> This dish was a favorite of mine even before I started working at America's Test Kitchen. Mac and cheese was a dish that was served a lot in my house—especially on meatless, Lenten Fridays. I was a very lucky kid—although I was more than happy to dine off mac and cheese from the famous "blue box," my mom more often would make a killer béchamel-based baked mac and cheese from scratch. This version is the first custard-based mac and cheese that I had ever tried, and still after 20 years, it's the version I cook in my kitchen at least once a month.

*bridget*

1  Bring 2 quarts water to boil in large pot. Add macaroni and 1 ½ teaspoons salt and cook, stirring often, until almost tender but still firm to the bite. Drain macaroni and leave it in colander.

2  Meanwhile, mix together eggs, half of evaporated milk, mustard mixture, hot sauce, ½ teaspoon salt, and ¼ teaspoon pepper in medium bowl. Set aside.

3  Return macaroni to pot. Set pot over low heat, add butter, and stir until melted.

4  Stir in egg mixture and 1 ½ cups cheddar. Continue to cook over low heat, gradually stirring in remaining evaporated milk and remaining 1 ½ cups cheddar, until mixture is hot and creamy, about 5 minutes. Season with salt and pepper to taste, and serve.

# spicy basil noodles with crispy tofu, snap peas, and bell pepper

serves 4

During my culinary school training, I had a 15-week externship at the Canyon Ranch health spa in the Berkshires. I started working on the salad bar station; it was one of the lowest, but busiest, jobs in the kitchen. Not only did I learn how to prep 15 cases of fruit and produce in about an hour, but I also started eating tofu. There was a simple appetizer that I had to prepare every day and I ate a lot of it while I worked. Now I really enjoy eating tofu, as long as it is prepared well. I especially love it fried and tossed with noodles, as in this recipe. Coating the tofu with a thin layer of cornstarch enables it to achieve a supercrisp texture. Plus, the sauce is like a flavor punch, with lots of spicy chiles, fish sauce, and lime juice. I usually add some of the chile seeds to make this dish good and spicy. You can't substitute other types of noodles, but you can use thinner (¼-inch-wide) dried flat rice noodles and reduce the soaking time to 20 minutes. "

*julia*

12 ounces (⅜-inch-wide) rice noodles

14 ounces extra-firm tofu, cut into 1-inch cubes

8 Thai, serrano, or jalapeño chiles, stemmed and seeded

4 shallots, peeled

6 garlic cloves, peeled

2 cups chicken broth

¼ cup fish sauce

¼ cup packed brown sugar

3 tablespoons lime juice (2 limes)

Salt and pepper

½ cup cornstarch

7 tablespoons vegetable oil

6 ounces sugar snap peas, strings removed

1 red bell pepper, stemmed, seeded, sliced into ¼-inch-wide strips, and halved crosswise

2 cups fresh Thai basil leaves or sweet basil leaves

1  Cover noodles with very hot tap water in large bowl and stir to separate. Let noodles soak until softened, pliable, and limp but not fully tender, 35 to 40 minutes; drain. Spread tofu out over paper towel–lined baking sheet and let drain for 20 minutes.

2  Meanwhile, pulse chiles, shallots, and garlic in food processor into smooth paste, about 30 pulses, scraping down bowl as needed; set aside. In bowl, whisk broth, fish sauce, sugar, and lime juice together.

3  Adjust oven rack to upper-middle position and heat oven to 200 degrees. Gently pat tofu dry with paper towels, season with salt and pepper, then toss with cornstarch in bowl. Transfer coated tofu to strainer and shake gently over bowl to remove excess cornstarch. Heat 3 tablespoons oil in 12-inch nonstick skillet over medium-high heat until just smoking. Add tofu and cook, turning as needed, until all sides are crisp and browned, about 8 minutes; transfer to paper towel–lined plate and keep warm in oven.

**4** Wipe out now-empty skillet with paper towels, add 1 tablespoon oil, and heat over high heat until just smoking. Add snap peas and bell pepper and cook, stirring often, until vegetables are crisp-tender and beginning to brown, 3 to 5 minutes; transfer to separate bowl.

**5** Add remaining 3 tablespoons oil to now-empty skillet and heat over medium-high heat until shimmering. Add processed chile mixture and cook until moisture evaporates and color deepens, 3 to 5 minutes. Add drained noodles and broth mixture and cook, tossing gently, until sauce has thickened and noodles are well coated and tender, 5 to 10 minutes.

**6** Stir in cooked vegetables and basil and cook until basil wilts slightly, about 1 minute. Top individual portions with crispy tofu and serve.

# stir-fried chicken with bok choy and crispy noodle cake

serves 4

### sauce

¼ cup chicken broth

2 tablespoons soy sauce

1 tablespoon dry sherry

1 tablespoon oyster sauce

1 teaspoon sugar

1 teaspoon cornstarch

¼ teaspoon red pepper flakes

### noodle cake

1 (9-ounce) package fresh Chinese noodles

1 teaspoon salt

2 scallions, sliced thin

¼ cup vegetable oil

### chicken stir-fry

1 pound boneless, skinless chicken breasts, trimmed and sliced thin

1 tablespoon soy sauce

1 tablespoon dry sherry

2 tablespoons toasted sesame oil

1 tablespoon cornstarch

1 tablespoon all-purpose flour

2 tablespoons plus 2 teaspoons vegetable oil

1 tablespoon grated fresh ginger

1 garlic clove, minced

1 pound bok choy, stalks cut on bias into ¼-inch slices, greens cut into ½-inch-wide strips

1 small red bell pepper, stemmed, seeded, and cut into ¼-inch-wide strips

**1 For the sauce** Whisk all ingredients together in small bowl; set aside.

**2 For the noodle cake** Bring 6 quarts water to boil in large pot. Add noodles and salt and cook, stirring often, until almost tender, 2 to 3 minutes. Drain noodles, then toss with scallions.

**3** Heat 2 tablespoons oil in 12-inch nonstick skillet over medium heat until shimmering. Spread noodles evenly across bottom of skillet and press with spatula to flatten. Cook until bottom of cake is crispy and golden brown, 5 to 8 minutes.

**4** Slide noodle cake onto large plate. Add remaining 2 tablespoons oil to skillet and swirl to coat. Invert noodle cake onto second plate and slide, browned side up, back into skillet. Cook until golden brown on second side, 5 to 8 minutes.

**5** Slide noodle cake onto cutting board and let sit for at least 5 minutes before slicing into wedges. (Noodle cake can be transferred to wire rack set in rimmed baking sheet and kept warm in 200-degree oven for up to 20 minutes.) Wipe skillet clean with paper towels.

**6 For the chicken stir-fry** While noodles boil, toss chicken with soy sauce and sherry in large bowl and let sit for at least 10 minutes or up to 1 hour. Whisk sesame oil, cornstarch, and flour together in large bowl. Combine 1 teaspoon vegetable oil, ginger, and garlic in small bowl.

7  Transfer chicken to cornstarch mixture. Heat 2 teaspoons vegetable oil in now-empty skillet over high heat until just smoking. Add half of chicken, breaking up any clumps, and cook without stirring until meat is browned around edges, about 1 minute. Stir chicken and continue to cook until cooked through, about 1 minute longer. Transfer chicken to clean, dry large bowl and cover with aluminum foil. Repeat with 2 teaspoons vegetable oil and remaining chicken.

8  Heat remaining 1 tablespoon vegetable oil in again-empty skillet over high heat until just smoking. Add bok choy stalks and bell pepper and cook until lightly browned, 2 to 3 minutes.

9  Push vegetables to sides of skillet. Add ginger mixture to center and cook, mashing mixture into pan, until fragrant, about 30 seconds. Stir mixture into vegetables. Add bok choy greens and cook until beginning to wilt, about 30 seconds.

10  Add chicken with any accumulated juices. Whisk sauce to recombine, then add to skillet and cook, tossing constantly, until sauce is thickened, about 30 seconds. Transfer to platter and serve with noodle cake.

# spicy sichuan noodles

serves 4

8 ounces ground pork

3 tablespoons soy sauce

2 tablespoons Chinese rice wine or dry sherry

White pepper

¼ cup peanut butter or Asian sesame paste

2 tablespoons oyster sauce

1 tablespoon rice vinegar

1¼ cups chicken broth

1 tablespoon vegetable oil

6 garlic cloves, minced

1 tablespoon grated fresh ginger

¾ teaspoon red pepper flakes

1 tablespoon toasted sesame oil

12 ounces dried Chinese noodles, 1 pound fresh Chinese noodles, or 12 ounces dried linguine

4 ounces (2 cups) bean sprouts (optional)

3 scallions, sliced thin

1 tablespoon Sichuan peppercorns, toasted and ground (optional)

"

I know that chicken noodle soup is great for when one isn't feeling well, but I prefer to slurp on a bowl of these Sichuan noodles. They're huge on flavor–salty, umami-rich soy sauce and oyster sauce plus the flavors of peanut and sesame will wake up the most dulled of palates. And if you need a sinus-buster, plenty of fresh garlic, ginger, and red pepper flakes are ready for the job. I've made lots of ingredient swaps depending on what I have handy and you can't go wrong. But I would consider the toasted and ground Sichuan pepper-corns a must. "

*bridget*

1  Combine pork, 1 tablespoon soy sauce, rice wine, and pinch white pepper in small bowl; stir well and set aside. Whisk peanut butter, oyster sauce, vinegar, pinch white pepper, and remaining 2 tablespoons soy sauce together in medium bowl. Whisk in broth and set aside.

2  Bring 4 quarts water to boil in large pot. Meanwhile, heat 12-inch skillet over high heat, add vegetable oil, and swirl to coat. Add pork mixture and cook, breaking into small pieces with wooden spoon, until well browned, about 5 minutes. Add garlic, ginger, and pepper flakes and cook, stirring constantly, until fragrant, about 1 minute. Add peanut butter mixture and bring to boil, whisking to combine, then reduce heat to medium-low and simmer, stirring occasionally, until flavors have blended, about 3 minutes. Stir in sesame oil.

3  While sauce simmers, add noodles to boiling water and cook until tender, 4 to 5 minutes for fresh or about 10 minutes for dried. Drain noodles and divide evenly among bowls. Ladle sauce over noodles and sprinkle with bean sprouts, if using; scallions; and Sichuan peppercorns, if using. Serve immediately.

# cold soba noodle salad

serves 4

"

I'm always making Marta eat new things (just a bite, at least). Many new foods don't go over so well, but soba noodles passed her taste test with flying colors. This simple cold noodle soba salad is our go-to recipe and since it is served cold, it works well for food on the go (aka car picnics) and for packed lunches. I love the spicy flavor of the radishes and wasabi, but am sure to tone these flavors down for Marta. I also like to toss in a few extra vegetables, such as edamame, shredded carrots, and thinly sliced cucumbers. For me, the distinct, smoky flavor of the bonito flakes are not optional; they're crucial to the dish. You can find nori and bonito flakes in the international aisle at the supermarket, or at an Asian market or a natural foods market. I don't recommend substituting other types of noodles for the soba noodles here. "

*julia*

14 ounces dried soba noodles

Salt

1 tablespoon vegetable oil

¼ cup soy sauce

3 tablespoons mirin

½ teaspoon sugar

½ teaspoon grated fresh ginger

¼ teaspoon wasabi paste or powder

4 large red radishes, trimmed and shredded

2 scallions, sliced thin on bias

1 (8 by 2½-inch) piece nori, cut into matchsticks with scissors

¼ cup dried bonito flakes (optional)

1  Bring 4 quarts water to boil in large pot. Add noodles and 1 tablespoon salt and cook, stirring often, until tender. Drain noodles, rinse with cold water, and drain again, leaving noodles slightly wet. Transfer to large bowl and toss with oil.

2  Whisk soy sauce, mirin, sugar, ginger, and wasabi together in small bowl, then pour over noodles. Add radishes and scallions and toss to combine. Divide noodles among individual bowls. Sprinkle each bowl with nori and bonito flakes, if using, and serve.

# southeast asian spring rolls with peanut sauce

makes 8 spring rolls

2½ tablespoons lime juice (2 limes)

1½ tablespoons fish sauce

1 teaspoon sugar

3 ounces rice vermicelli

1 large carrot, peeled and shredded

⅓ cup dry-roasted peanuts, chopped

1 jalapeño chile or 2 Thai chiles, stemmed, seeded, and minced, or ½ teaspoon red pepper flakes

1 large cucumber, peeled, halved lengthwise, seeded, and cut into 2-inch matchsticks

4 leaves red leaf lettuce or Boston lettuce, halved lengthwise

8 (8-inch) round rice paper wrappers

½ cup fresh Thai basil or mint, small leaves left whole, medium and large leaves torn into ½-inch pieces

½ cup fresh cilantro leaves

8 ounces cooked extra-large shrimp (21 to 25 per pound), chilled and sliced in half lengthwise

1 recipe Peanut Dipping Sauce (recipe follows)

1   Combine lime juice, fish sauce, and sugar in small bowl.

2   Bring 1½ quarts water to boil in kettle or saucepan. Place noodles in bowl. Pour boiling water over noodles. Stir, then soak until noodles are tender but not mushy, 12 to 14 minutes, stirring once halfway through soaking. Drain noodles, transfer to medium bowl, add 2 tablespoons fish sauce mixture, and toss to coat.

3   Combine carrot, peanuts, and jalapeño in small bowl. Add 1 tablespoon fish sauce mixture and toss to combine. Toss cucumber with remaining 1 tablespoon fish sauce mixture in second small bowl.

4   Place lettuce on platter. Spread clean, damp dish towel on counter. Fill 9-inch pie plate with 1 inch room-temperature water. Immerse 1 wrapper in water until just pliable, about 2 minutes; lay softened wrapper on towel. Scatter about 6 basil leaves and 6 cilantro leaves over wrapper. Arrange 5 cucumber matchsticks horizontally on wrapper and top with 1 tablespoon carrot mixture. Arrange about 2½ tablespoons noodles on top of carrot mixture and top with 2 shrimp halves. Fold bottom 2-inch border of wrapper up over filling. Fold left edge, then right edge of wrapper over filling. Roll to top edge of wrapper to form tight cylinder. Set roll on 1 lettuce piece on platter. Cover with second damp dish towel. Repeat soaking and rolling with remaining wrappers and filling. Serve with peanut dipping sauce, wrapping lettuce around exterior of each roll. (Spring rolls are best eaten immediately, but they can be held for up to 4 hours in refrigerator, covered with clean, damp dish towel.)

## peanut dipping sauce
makes about ¾ cup

¼ cup creamy peanut butter

¼ cup hoisin sauce

¼ cup water

2 tablespoons tomato paste

1 teaspoon Asian chili-garlic sauce (optional)

2 teaspoons peanut oil or vegetable oil

2 garlic cloves, minced

1 teaspoon red pepper flakes

Whisk peanut butter, hoisin, water, tomato paste, and chili-garlic sauce, if using, together in small bowl. Heat oil, garlic, and pepper flakes in small saucepan over medium heat until fragrant, 1 to 2 minutes. Stir in peanut butter mixture, bring to simmer, then reduce heat to medium-low and cook, stirring occasionally, until flavors have blended, about 3 minutes. (Sauce should have ketchup-like consistency; if too thick, add water, 1 teaspoon at a time, until proper consistency is reached.) Transfer sauce to bowl and let cool completely. (Sauce can be refrigerated for up to 3 days. Bring to room temperature before serving.)

# thai pork lettuce wraps

serves 6 as appetizer or 4 as main course

1 (1-pound) pork tenderloin, trimmed and cut into 1-inch chunks

2½ tablespoons fish sauce

1 tablespoon white rice

¼ cup chicken broth

2 shallots, peeled and sliced into thin rings

3 tablespoons lime juice (2 limes)

3 tablespoons coarsely chopped fresh mint

3 tablespoons coarsely chopped fresh cilantro

2 teaspoons sugar

¼ teaspoon red pepper flakes

1 head Bibb lettuce (8 ounces), leaves separated and left whole

" This is the dish that you need to make if you want to get a picky eater to try lettuce. I first made this dish for my boys with tender chunks of pork tenderloin, and at the dinner table, we competed for who could make the biggest 'crunch' with their lettuce wraps. From there we tried other types of lettuce (romaine: OK crunch, iceberg: HUGE crunch) and it was a good way to let the kids experiment with food. Nowadays, the kids will eat almost any food wrapped in lettuce! "

*bridget*

1  Place pork chunks on large plate in single layer. Freeze pork until firm and starting to harden around edges but still pliable, 15 to 20 minutes. Working with half of semifrozen meat at a time, pulse in food processor until coarsely chopped, about 5 pulses; transfer to bowl. Toss meat with 1 tablespoon fish sauce, cover, and refrigerate for 15 minutes.

2  Toast rice in 8-inch skillet over medium-high heat, stirring constantly, until deep golden brown, about 5 minutes. Transfer rice to small bowl, let cool for 5 minutes, then grind into fine meal using spice grinder (10 to 30 seconds) or mortar and pestle.

3  Bring broth to simmer in 12-inch nonstick skillet over medium-high heat. Add marinated pork and cook, stirring frequently, until pork is about half-pink, about 2 minutes. Sprinkle 1 teaspoon rice powder into skillet and cook, stirring constantly, until pork is no longer pink, 1 to 1½ minutes longer.

4  Transfer pork to large bowl and let cool for 10 minutes. Stir in remaining 1½ tablespoons fish sauce, remaining 2 teaspoons rice powder, shallots, lime juice, mint, cilantro, sugar, and pepper flakes and toss to combine. Serve with lettuce leaves.

# rustic potato-leek soup with kielbasa

serves 4

1 (12-inch) baguette, sliced 1 inch thick on bias

1 garlic clove, peeled

2 tablespoons extra-virgin olive oil

4 tablespoons unsalted butter

8 ounces kielbasa sausage, halved lengthwise and sliced ½ inch thick

2 pounds leeks, white and light green parts only, halved lengthwise, sliced 1 inch thick, and washed thoroughly

5 cups chicken broth

8 ounces red potatoes, unpeeled, cut into ¾-inch pieces

Salt and pepper

"

One of the first things Ian and I tried to cook together when we met (he's a terrific cook) was a simple potato and leek soup. I had a rustic soup in mind, such as this recipe, while he wanted a classic pureed version. We compromised and wound up with a bland pureed potato soup garnished with limp, noodle-like pieces of leeks. Upon eating it, we both laughed, agreed that it was pretty terrible, and ordered a pizza. I like the smooth, pureed versions of this classic soup well enough, but I much prefer this hearty, brothy, rustic style along with the garlic-flavored toasts for dinner. It reminds me of soups my mother made when I was growing up. When prepping the leeks, I always cut them first and then wash them using a salad spinner to get rid of all the sandy grit before cooking. "

*julia*

1  Adjust oven rack to middle position and heat oven to 400 degrees. Arrange bread in single layer on rimmed baking sheet and bake until dry and crisp, about 10 minutes, turning slices over halfway through baking. While still hot, rub each slice of bread with garlic and drizzle with oil; set aside.

2  Meanwhile, melt butter in Dutch oven over medium heat. Cook kielbasa until lightly browned, 2 to 3 minutes. Stir in leeks, cover, and cook, stirring occasionally, until leeks are tender but not mushy, 10 to 15 minutes.

3  Stir in broth, scraping up any browned bits. Stir in potatoes and bring to simmer. Cover, reduce heat to medium-low, and simmer gently until potatoes are almost tender, 5 to 7 minutes.

4  Off heat, let sit until potatoes are tender and flavors meld, 10 to 15 minutes. Season with salt and pepper to taste, and serve with garlic toast.

# broccoli-cheese soup

serves 6 to 8

2 tablespoons unsalted butter

2 pounds broccoli, florets chopped into 1-inch pieces, stalks peeled and sliced ¼ inch thick

1 onion, chopped coarse

2 garlic cloves, minced

1½ teaspoons dry mustard

Pinch cayenne pepper

Salt and pepper

3-4 cups water

¼ teaspoon baking soda

2 cups chicken broth

2 ounces (2 cups) baby spinach

3 ounces sharp cheddar cheese, shredded (¾ cup)

1½ ounces Parmesan cheese, grated fine (¾ cup), plus extra for serving

1 recipe Butter Croutons (recipe follows)

1 Melt butter in Dutch oven over medium-high heat. Add broccoli, onion, garlic, mustard, cayenne, and 1 teaspoon salt and cook, stirring frequently, until fragrant, about 6 minutes. Add 1 cup water and baking soda. Bring to simmer, cover, and cook until broccoli is very soft, about 20 minutes, stirring once during cooking.

2 Add broth and 2 cups water and increase heat to medium-high. When mixture begins to simmer, stir in spinach and cook until wilted, about 1 minute. Transfer half of soup to blender, add cheddar and Parmesan, and process until smooth, about 1 minute. Transfer soup to medium bowl and repeat with remaining soup. Return soup to Dutch oven, place over medium heat and bring to simmer. Adjust consistency of soup with up to 1 cup water. Season with salt and pepper to taste. Serve, sprinkling with croutons and passing extra Parmesan.

"

I used to bellyache about the high price of broccoli–before I started to grow my own. Every year, my broccoli plants seemed to be growing beautifully with full, yellow-green crowns forming on sturdy, healthy stalks. The hardest part was knowing when to harvest. Pick too soon and the broccoli won't be full flavored, wait too long, and the plants start to flower, which makes the broccoli incredibly bitter. So, knowing my limitations, I now buy my perfectly emerald-green broccoli from local farmers and concentrate on making a hearty-but-not-heavy broccoli cheese soup. And yes, thanks to a little spinach, this soup is beautifully green too. "

*bridget*

### butter croutons

makes about 3 cups

6 slices hearty white sandwich bread, crusts removed, cut into ½-inch cubes (about 3 cups)

Salt and pepper

3 tablespoons unsalted butter, melted

1  Adjust oven rack to upper-middle position and heat oven to 350 degrees. Combine bread cubes and salt and pepper to taste in medium bowl. Drizzle with melted butter and toss well using rubber spatula to combine.

2  Spread bread cubes in single layer on rimmed baking sheet or in shallow baking dish. Bake croutons until golden brown and crisp, 8 to 10 minutes, stirring halfway through baking. Let cool on baking sheet to room temperature. (Croutons can be stored in airtight container for up to 3 days.)

137

# pasta Os with mini meatballs

serves 4

1 tablespoon olive oil

1 onion, chopped fine

1 carrot, peeled and chopped fine

3 garlic cloves, minced

3½ cups chicken broth

1 (28-ounce) can diced tomatoes

8 ounces meatloaf mix

¼ cup prepared basil pesto

¼ cup panko bread crumbs

Salt and pepper

4 ounces (1 cup) ditalini

"

Marta is a big fan of SpaghettiOs, as was I at her age. Yet I'm not a fan of all the junk inside those prepared cans, including a surprising amount of sugar and sodium. Enter this homemade recipe, which is not only a cinch to make but has a simple, tomatoey flavor that all of us love. It's a perfect Saturday lunch when the weather outside is a bit chilly. I usually double the recipe and freeze some for later (without the noodles); having it in the freezer is like having gold in the bank. Sometimes, if the sauce is looking a bit thick, I thin it out with some water or broth as the noodles are cooking. We like to serve this with warm garlic bread. "

*julia*

1  Cook oil, onion, and carrot in Dutch oven over medium heat until vegetables are softened, about 5 minutes. Stir in garlic and cook until fragrant, about 30 seconds. Stir in broth and tomatoes and their juice. Simmer until vegetables are tender, about 10 minutes.

2  Meanwhile, using your hands, mix meatloaf mix, pesto, panko, ⅛ teaspoon salt, and ⅛ teaspoon pepper in bowl until uniform. Pinch off heaping teaspoons of meat mixture and roll into ¾-inch meatballs (about 32 meatballs).

3  Working in batches, puree soup in blender until smooth and return to clean pot. Return to simmer, then stir in pasta and gently add meatballs. Continue to simmer, uncovered, until pasta is tender and meatballs are cooked through, 10 to 12 minutes. Off heat, season with salt and pepper to taste. Serve. (Soup can be refrigerated for up to 3 days; add water as needed when reheating to adjust consistency.)

# creamy cauliflower soup

serves 4 to 6

"

As a kid, cauliflower really creeped me out. My mom (an excellent cook) would baste a huge head of cauliflower with butter and saffron and then steam it in a big pot. When the dish was finished cooking, Mom would pull out something that closely resembled a human brain, as the deep orange-red hue from the saffron butter had settled into the crooks of the florets. Tasty? Yes. Creepy? You bet. Likewise, this blond soup isn't a looker, but the flavor is pure buttery, delicate cauliflower, with a little assist from creamy leeks. Two bits of advice: Double the soup—it freezes beautifully. Also, don't make the buttery, tangy cauliflower garnish too far in advance. It's a great snack and you'll have none left to serve with your soup. "

*bridget*

1 head cauliflower (2 pounds)

8 tablespoons unsalted butter, cut into 8 pieces

1 leek, white and light green parts only, halved lengthwise, sliced thin, and washed thoroughly

1 small onion, halved and sliced thin

Salt and pepper

4½-5 cups water

½ teaspoon sherry vinegar

3 tablespoons minced fresh chives

1  Pull off outer leaves of cauliflower and trim stem. Using paring knife, cut around core to remove; slice core thin and reserve. Cut heaping 1 cup of ½-inch florets from head of cauliflower; set aside. Cut remaining cauliflower crosswise into ½-inch-thick slices.

2  Melt 3 tablespoons butter in large saucepan over medium-low heat. Add leek, onion, and 1½ teaspoons salt. Cook, stirring often, until leek and onion are softened but not browned, about 7 minutes.

3  Add 4½ cups water, sliced core, and half of sliced cauliflower. Increase heat to medium-high and bring to simmer. Reduce heat to medium-low and simmer gently for 15 minutes. Add remaining sliced cauliflower and simmer until cauliflower is tender and crumbles easily, 15 to 20 minutes.

4  Meanwhile, melt remaining 5 tablespoons butter in 8-inch skillet over medium heat. Add reserved florets and cook, stirring often, until florets are golden brown and butter is browned and has nutty aroma, 6 to 8 minutes. Remove skillet from heat and use slotted spoon to transfer florets to small bowl. Toss florets with vinegar and season with salt to taste. Pour browned butter in skillet into separate bowl and reserve for garnishing.

5  Process soup in blender until smooth, about 45 seconds. Return pureed soup to clean pot, bring to brief simmer over medium heat, and adjust consistency with remaining water as needed (soup should have thick, velvety texture but should be thin enough to settle with flat surface after being stirred). Season with salt to taste. Serve, garnishing individual bowls with browned florets, drizzle of browned butter, chives, and pepper.

*Home-Style Dinners*

# black-eyed peas and greens

serves 6 to 8

6 slices bacon, cut into ½-inch pieces

1 onion, halved and sliced thin

1¼ teaspoons salt

4 garlic cloves, minced

½ teaspoon ground cumin

½ teaspoon pepper

¼ teaspoon red pepper flakes

1 (14.5-ounce) can diced tomatoes

1½ cups chicken broth

1 pound collard greens, stemmed and chopped

2 (15-ounce) cans black-eyed peas, rinsed

1 tablespoon cider vinegar

1 teaspoon sugar

"

OK folks, enough with the kale. It's time to move on to a much better (in my opinion) green–collards! Collard greens have gotten a bad rap over the years–probably due to the fact that folks thought that stewing them for hours was the best way to soften their flavor. Not so. Deeply earthy and unapologetically bitter collard greens soften in texture and bite with just a 30-minute simmer. I make sure to make this dish on New Year's Day, as it contains several 'lucky' ingredients. Pork (bacon) for prosperity and progress, greens, which symbol-ize paper money, and black-eyed peas, which resemble coins. I highly recom-mend spooning a serving over a bowl of crumbled cornbread and drizzling with a little pomegranate molasses instead of the cider vinegar. "

*bridget*

1  Cook bacon in Dutch oven over medium heat until crisp, 5 to 7 minutes. Transfer bacon to paper towel–lined plate; set aside.

2  Remove all but 2 tablespoons fat from pot. Add onion and salt and cook, stirring frequently, until golden brown, about 10 minutes. Add garlic, cumin, pepper, and pepper flakes and cook until fragrant, about 30 seconds.

3  Add tomatoes and their juice. Stir in broth and bring to boil. Add greens, cover, and reduce heat to medium-low. Simmer until greens are tender, about 15 minutes.

4  Add black-eyed peas to pot and cook, covered, stirring occasionally, until greens are silky and completely tender, about 15 minutes. Remove lid, increase heat to medium-high, and cook until liquid is reduced by one-fourth, about 5 minutes. Stir in vinegar and sugar. Top with reserved bacon. Serve.

# eggs in purgatory

serves 4

8 (¾-inch-thick) slices rustic Italian bread

7 tablespoons extra-virgin olive oil, plus extra for drizzling

4 garlic cloves, sliced thin

¼ cup grated onion

1 tablespoon tomato paste

¾–1¼ teaspoons red pepper flakes

Salt and pepper

½ teaspoon dried oregano

1 cup fresh basil leaves, plus 2 tablespoons chopped

1 (28-ounce) can crushed tomatoes

8 large eggs

¼ cup grated Parmesan cheese

1  Adjust oven rack to middle position and heat broiler. Arrange bread slices on baking sheet and drizzle first sides with 2 tablespoons oil; flip slices and drizzle with 2 tablespoons oil. Broil until deep golden brown, about 3 minutes per side. Set aside and heat oven to 400 degrees.

2  Heat remaining 3 tablespoons oil in ovensafe 12-inch skillet over medium heat until shimmering. Add garlic and cook until golden, about 2 minutes. Add onion, tomato paste, pepper flakes, 1 teaspoon salt, and oregano and cook, stirring occasionally, until rust-colored, about 4 minutes. Add basil leaves and cook until wilted, about 30 seconds. Stir in tomatoes and bring to gentle simmer. Reduce heat to medium-low and continue to simmer until slightly thickened, about 15 minutes, stirring occasionally.

3  Remove skillet from heat and let sit 2 minutes to cool slightly. Crack 1 egg into bowl. Use rubber spatula to clear 2-inch-diameter well in sauce, exposing skillet bottom. Using spatula to hold well open, immediately pour in egg. Repeat with remaining eggs, evenly spacing 7 eggs in total around perimeter of skillet and 1 egg in center.

4  Season each egg with salt and pepper. Cook over medium heat, covered, until egg whites are just beginning to set but are still translucent with some watery patches, about 3 minutes. Uncover skillet and transfer to oven. Bake until egg whites are set and no watery patches remain, 4 to 5 minutes for slightly runny yolks or about 6 minutes for soft-cooked yolks, rotating skillet halfway through baking.

5  Sprinkle with Parmesan and chopped basil and drizzle with extra oil. Serve with toasted bread.

# quinoa patties with spinach and sun-dried tomatoes

serves 4

½ cup oil-packed sun-dried tomatoes, chopped coarse, plus 1 tablespoon packing oil

4 scallions, chopped fine

4 garlic cloves, minced

2 cups water

1 cup prewashed quinoa

1 teaspoon salt

2 slices hearty white sandwich bread

1 large egg plus 1 large yolk, beaten

½ teaspoon grated lemon zest plus 2 teaspoons juice

2 ounces (2 cups) baby spinach, chopped

2 ounces Parmesan cheese, grated (1 cup)

2 tablespoons vegetable oil

1 recipe Cucumber-Yogurt Sauce (recipe follows)

> I've loved quinoa for years, but I never got very creative with it at home beyond a simple side dish. Lucky for me, quinoa became a 'superfood' a few years back, earning it serious fame and worldwide popularity. With all this attention, quinoa became a bit of a muse for us in the test kitchen and we challenged ourselves to find new ways to bring it to the table. We've since used it to add crunch to a granola and cobbler topping, built stews and soups around it, and even turned it into a breakfast porridge. Of all the quinoa recipes we've come up with, these quinoa patties are my favorite by far. The outside cooks to a crisp shell around a soft, creamy interior.

*julia*

1  Line rimmed baking sheet with parchment paper. Heat tomato oil in large saucepan over medium heat until shimmering. Add scallions and cook until softened, 3 to 5 minutes. Stir in garlic and cook until fragrant, about 30 seconds. Stir in water, quinoa, and salt and bring to simmer. Cover, reduce heat to medium-low, and simmer until quinoa is tender, 16 to 18 minutes. Off heat, let quinoa sit, covered, until liquid is fully absorbed, about 10 minutes. Transfer quinoa to large bowl and let cool for 15 minutes.

2  Pulse bread in food processor until coarsely ground, about 10 pulses. Add egg and yolk and lemon zest and pulse until mixture comes together, about 5 pulses. Stir bread mixture, tomatoes, lemon juice, spinach, and Parmesan into cooled quinoa until thoroughly combined. Divide mixture into 8 equal portions, pack firmly into ½-inch-thick patties (about 3½ inches wide), and place on prepared sheet. Cover and refrigerate patties for at least 1 hour or up to 24 hours.

3  Heat 1 tablespoon vegetable oil in 12-inch nonstick skillet over medium-low heat until shimmering. Gently lay 4 patties in skillet and cook until well browned on first side, 5 to 7 minutes. Gently flip patties and continue to cook until golden brown on second side, 5 to 7 minutes. Transfer patties to serving platter and tent with aluminum foil. Return now-empty skillet to medium-low heat and repeat with remaining 1 tablespoon vegetable oil and remaining 4 patties. Serve with Cucumber-Yogurt Sauce.

## cucumber-yogurt sauce
makes about 1¼ cups

½ cup plain Greek yogurt

1 tablespoon extra-virgin olive oil

1 tablespoon minced fresh dill

1 small garlic clove, minced

½ cucumber, peeled, halved lengthwise, seeded, and shredded

Salt and pepper

Whisk yogurt, oil, dill, and garlic together in medium bowl. Stir in cucumber and season with salt and pepper to taste. (Sauce can be refrigerated for up to 1 day.)

# casual
# entertaining

# patatas bravas

serves 4 to 6

## sauce

1 tablespoon vegetable oil

2 teaspoons garlic, minced to paste

1 teaspoon smoked paprika

½ teaspoon kosher salt

½–¾ teaspoon cayenne pepper

¼ cup tomato paste

2 teaspoons sherry vinegar

¼ cup mayonnaise

## potatoes

2¼ pounds russet potatoes, peeled and cut into 1-inch pieces

½ teaspoon baking soda

Kosher salt

3 cups vegetable oil

1  **For the sauce**  Heat oil in small saucepan over medium-low heat until shimmering. Add garlic, paprika, salt, and cayenne and cook until fragrant, about 30 seconds. Add tomato paste and cook for 30 seconds. Whisk in ½ cup water and bring to boil over high heat. Reduce heat to medium-low and simmer until slightly thickened, 4 to 5 minutes. Transfer sauce to bowl, stir in vinegar, and let cool completely. Once cool, whisk in mayonnaise. (Sauce can be refrigerated for up to 24 hours. Bring to room temperature before serving.)

2  **For the potatoes**  Bring 8 cups water to boil in large saucepan over high heat. Add potatoes and baking soda. Return to boil and cook for 1 minute. Drain potatoes.

3  Return potatoes to saucepan and place over low heat. Cook, shaking saucepan occasionally, until any surface moisture has evaporated, 30 seconds to 1 minute. Remove from heat. Add 1 ½ teaspoons salt and stir with rubber spatula until potatoes are coated with thick, starchy paste, about 30 seconds. Transfer potatoes to rimmed baking sheet in single layer to cool. (Potatoes can stand at room temperature for up to 2 hours.)

4  Heat oil in large Dutch oven over high heat to 375 degrees. Set wire rack in rimmed baking sheet and line with paper towels. Add all potatoes to oil (they should just be submerged) and cook, stirring occasionally with wire skimmer or slotted spoon, until deep golden brown and crispy, 20 to 25 minutes.

5  Transfer potatoes to prepared rack and season with salt to taste. Spoon ½ cup sauce onto bottom of large platter or 1 ½ tablespoons sauce onto individual plates. Arrange potatoes over sauce and serve immediately, passing remaining sauce separately.

*Casual Entertaining*

# muhammara

makes about 2 cups

1½ cups jarred roasted red peppers, rinsed and patted dry

1 cup walnuts, toasted

¼ cup plain wheat crackers, crumbled

3 tablespoons pomegranate molasses

2 tablespoons extra-virgin olive oil

Salt

½ teaspoon ground cumin

Cayenne pepper

Lemon juice, as needed

1 tablespoon minced fresh parsley (optional)

Pulse red peppers, walnuts, crackers, pomegranate molasses, oil, ¾ teaspoon salt, cumin, and ⅛ teaspoon cayenne in food processor until smooth, about 10 pulses. Transfer to serving bowl, cover, and refrigerate for 15 minutes. (Dip can be refrigerated for up to 24 hours; bring to room temperature before serving.) Season with lemon juice, salt, and cayenne to taste, and sprinkle with parsley, if using, before serving.

"

I developed this recipe about 13 years ago for one of our cookbooks and I still make it all the time. The combination of roasted red peppers, walnuts, and pomegranate molasses seemed downright exotic to me back then, even though I swapped regular old bell peppers for the traditional Aleppo peppers. I like using jarred roasted red peppers because they're such a timesaver, but I do roast my own peppers when I have time because it gives the dip a fresher, cleaner flavor. Bread is a standard muhammara ingredient, but I prefer the flavor and sweetness that crushed wheat crackers add; I usually use Carr's Whole Wheat Crackers. "

*julia*

# steamed chinese dumplings

serves 8 to 10

2 tablespoons soy sauce

½ teaspoon unflavored gelatin

1 pound boneless country-style pork ribs, cut into 1-inch pieces

8 ounces shrimp, peeled and deveined, tails removed, halved lengthwise

¼ cup chopped water chestnuts

4 dried shiitake mushroom caps (about ¾ ounce), soaked in hot water for 30 minutes, squeezed dry, and chopped fine

2 tablespoons cornstarch

2 tablespoons minced fresh cilantro

1 tablespoon toasted sesame oil

1 tablespoon Chinese rice wine or dry sherry

1 tablespoon rice vinegar

2 teaspoons sugar

2 teaspoons grated fresh ginger

½ teaspoon salt

½ teaspoon pepper

1 (1-pound) package 5½-inch square egg roll wrappers

¼ cup finely grated carrot (optional)

Chili oil

1  Combine soy sauce and gelatin in small bowl. Set aside to allow gelatin to bloom, about 5 minutes.

2  Meanwhile, pulse half of pork in food processor until coarsely ground into ⅛-inch pieces, about 10 pulses; transfer to large bowl. Add shrimp and remaining pork to food processor and pulse until coarsely chopped into ¼-inch pieces, about 5 pulses. Add to finely ground pork. Stir in soy sauce mixture, water chestnuts, mushrooms, cornstarch, cilantro, sesame oil, wine, vinegar, sugar, ginger, salt, and pepper.

3  Divide egg roll wrappers into 3 stacks. Using 3-inch biscuit cutter, cut two rounds from each stack. Cover with moist paper towels to prevent drying.

4  Working with 6 rounds at a time, brush edges of each round lightly with water. Place heaping tablespoon of filling in center of each round. Form dumplings by pinching opposing sides of wrapper with your fingers until you have 8 equidistant pinches. Gather up sides of dumpling and squeeze gently to create "waist." Hold dumpling in your hand and gently but firmly pack down filling with butter knife. Transfer to parchment paper–lined baking sheet, cover with damp dish towel, and repeat with remaining wrappers and filling. Top center of each dumpling with pinch of grated carrot, if using.

5  Cut piece of parchment paper slightly smaller than diameter of steamer basket and place in basket. Poke about 20 small holes in parchment and lightly coat with vegetable oil spray. Place batches of dumplings on parchment, making sure they are not touching. Set steamer over simmering water and cook, covered, until no longer pink, 8 to 10 minutes. Serve immediately with chili oil.

# pissaladière

makes two 14 by 8-inch tarts, serving 4 to 6

Folks who ask me what my favorite foods or ingredients are will know that olives are near the top of that list, so I love when a recipe features those briny or cured little fruits. This pissaladière, with its crackly, chewy thin crust, caramelized onions, and minced anchovies, is perfect for slicing and serving to guests as an appetizer or snack. Pair it with a barely dressed salad, and you've got a perfect meal. One moderate modification: I crack the fennel seeds in a mortar and pestle, which opens their flavor even more. "

*bridget*

### dough

3 cups (16½ ounces) bread flour

2 teaspoons sugar

½ teaspoon instant or rapid-rise yeast

1⅓ cups ice water

1 tablespoon extra-virgin olive oil

1½ teaspoons salt

### toppings

¼ cup extra-virgin olive oil

2 pounds onions, halved and sliced ¼ inch thick

1 teaspoon packed brown sugar

½ teaspoon salt

1 tablespoon water

½ cup pitted niçoise olives, chopped coarse

8 anchovy fillets, rinsed, patted dry, and chopped coarse, plus 12 fillets for garnish (optional)

2 teaspoons minced fresh thyme

1 teaspoon fennel seeds

½ teaspoon pepper

2 tablespoons minced fresh parsley

1  **For the dough** Pulse flour, sugar, and yeast in food processor until combined, about 5 pulses. With processor running, slowly add ice water and process until dough is just combined and no dry flour remains, about 10 seconds. Let dough rest for 10 minutes.

2  Add oil and salt to dough and process until dough forms satiny, sticky ball that clears sides of bowl,

30 to 60 seconds. Transfer dough to lightly floured counter and knead by hand to form smooth, round ball, about 30 seconds. Place dough seam side down in lightly greased large bowl or container, cover tightly with plastic wrap, and refrigerate for at least 24 hours or up to 3 days.

3  **For the toppings** Heat 2 tablespoons oil in 12-inch nonstick skillet over medium heat until shimmering. Stir in onions, sugar, and salt. Cover and cook, stirring occasionally, until onions are softened and have released their juice, about 10 minutes. Remove lid and continue to cook, stirring often, until onions are golden brown, 10 to 15 minutes. Transfer onions to bowl, stir in water, and let cool completely before using.

4  One hour before baking, adjust oven rack 4 inches from broiler element, set baking stone on rack, and heat oven to 500 degrees. Press down on dough to deflate. Transfer dough to clean counter, divide in half, and cover loosely with greased plastic. Pat 1 piece of dough (keep remaining piece covered) into 4-inch round. Working around circumference of dough, fold edges toward center until ball forms.

5  Flip ball seam side down and, using your cupped hands, drag in small circles on counter until dough feels taut and round and all seams are secured on underside. (If dough sticks to your hands, lightly dust top of dough with flour.) Repeat with remaining piece of dough. Space

dough balls 3 inches apart, cover loosely with greased plastic, and let rest for 1 hour.

6 Heat broiler for 10 minutes. Meanwhile, generously coat 1 dough ball with flour and place on well-floured counter. Press and roll into 14 by 8-inch oval. Transfer oval to well-floured pizza peel and reshape as needed. (If dough resists stretching, let it relax for 10 to 20 minutes before trying to stretch it again.) Using fork, poke entire surface of oval 10 to 15 times.

7 Brush dough oval with 1 tablespoon oil, then sprinkle evenly with ¼ cup olives, half of chopped anchovies, 1 teaspoon thyme, ½ teaspoon fennel seeds, and ¼ teaspoon pepper, leaving ½-inch border around edge. Arrange half of onions on top, followed by 6 whole anchovies, if using.

8 Slide flatbread carefully onto baking stone and return oven to 500 degrees. Bake until bottom crust is evenly browned and edges are crisp, 13 to 15 minutes, rotating flatbread halfway through baking. Transfer flatbread to wire rack and let cool for 5 minutes. Sprinkle with 1 tablespoon parsley, slice, and serve. Heat broiler for 10 minutes. Repeat with remaining dough, oil, and toppings, returning oven to 500 degrees when flatbread is placed on stone.

# homemade cheese straws

serves 4 to 6

1 (9½ by 9-inch) sheet puff pastry, thawed

2 ounces Parmesan or aged Asiago cheese, grated (1 cup)

1 tablespoon minced fresh parsley

¼ teaspoon salt

⅛ teaspoon pepper

" These easy straws taste so much better than any you can buy at the store. I love serving them with soup, such as tomato soup or gazpacho. Using store-bought puff pastry made with all butter, such as Dufour brand, makes a difference if you can find it; otherwise, Pepperidge Farm Puff Pastry works fine. Also, I've found that the unbaked straws can be frozen for several weeks before baking. Once you get the hang of the method, it's easy to swap in other types of cheese and add some fun seasonings, like mustard seeds, fennel seeds, and pink peppercorns. Be sure to allow enough time to defrost the puff pastry. To thaw frozen puff pastry, let it sit in the refrigerator for 24 hours or on the counter for 30 minutes to 1 hour. "

*julia*

1 Adjust oven rack to middle position and heat oven to 425 degrees. Line rimmed baking sheet with parchment paper.

2 Lay puff pastry on second sheet of parchment and sprinkle with Parmesan, parsley, salt, and pepper. Top with third sheet of parchment. Using rolling pin, press cheese mixture into pastry, then roll pastry into 10-inch square.

3 Remove top sheet of parchment and cut pastry into thirteen ¾-inch-wide strips with sharp knife or pizza wheel. Gently twist each strip of pastry and space about ½ inch apart on prepared baking sheet.

4 Bake until cheese straws are fully puffed and golden brown, 10 to 15 minutes. Let cheese straws cool completely on baking sheet. Serve.

# the best fresh margaritas

makes about 4 cups; serves 4 to 6

4 teaspoons finely grated lime zest plus ½ cup juice (4 limes)

4 teaspoons finely grated lemon zest plus ½ cup juice (3 lemons)

¼ cup superfine sugar

Pinch salt

2 cups crushed ice

1 cup 100 percent agave tequila, preferably reposado

1 cup triple sec

1  Combine lime zest and juice, lemon zest and juice, sugar, and salt in 2-cup liquid measuring cup. Cover and refrigerate until flavors meld, at least 4 hours or up to 24 hours.

2  Divide 1 cup crushed ice among 4 to 6 margarita or double old-fashioned glasses. Strain juice mixture into 1-quart pitcher or cocktail shaker; discard solids. Add tequila, triple sec, and remaining 1 cup crushed ice; stir or shake until thoroughly combined and chilled, 20 to 60 seconds. Strain into ice-filled glasses and serve immediately.

> Ah… one of my proudest moments in the test kitchen was when I developed this recipe so many years ago. I can't tell you how difficult the testing was—having to drink sample after sample of margarita test batches. Look, it's a hard job but I was willing to do it, and I think that this margarita recipe is pretty fantastic. One thing I've learned since then: You can make the entire margarita a day in advance, which I think softens the tequila just a bit. Before you strain out the zests, pour in the tequila and triple sec and refrigerate the margaritas for up to a day, then strain before serving. This drink's on me.

*bridget*

# spanakopita

serves 10 to 12

Sometimes I invent reasons to make this recipe for spanakopita, because it serves too many people to make it just for myself. There's just something about the flavor of the spinach with the yogurt, feta, mint, and dill that I find soothing and somewhat addictive. The problem with most spanakopitas is that the pastry gets soggy and the spinach doesn't have enough flavor—not with this version. Over the years, I've found it increasingly hard to find bags of curly-leaf spinach, but bunches of flat-leaf spinach work fine as a substitute; baby spinach will not work here. ”

*julia*

*filling*

20 ounces curly-leaf spinach, stemmed

8 ounces feta cheese, crumbled (2 cups)

¾ cup whole-milk Greek yogurt

4 scallions, sliced thin

2 large eggs, lightly beaten

¼ cup minced fresh mint

2 tablespoons minced fresh dill

3 garlic cloves, minced

1 teaspoon grated lemon zest plus 1 tablespoon juice

1 teaspoon ground nutmeg

½ teaspoon pepper

¼ teaspoon salt

⅛ teaspoon cayenne pepper

*phyllo layers*

7 tablespoons extra-virgin olive oil

8 ounces (14 by 9-inch) phyllo, thawed

1½ ounces Pecorino Romano cheese, grated (¾ cup)

2 teaspoons sesame seeds (optional)

1  **For the filling**  Place spinach and ¼ cup water in bowl. Cover and microwave until spinach is wilted and volume is halved, about 5 minutes. Remove bowl from microwave and keep covered for 1 minute. Transfer spinach to colander and gently press to release liquid. Transfer spinach to cutting board and chop coarse. Return to colander and press again. Stir spinach, feta, yogurt, scallions, eggs, mint, dill, garlic, lemon zest and juice, nutmeg, pepper, salt, and cayenne in bowl until thoroughly combined.

2  **For the phyllo layers**  Adjust oven rack to lower-middle position and heat oven to 425 degrees. Line rimmed baking sheet with parchment paper. Using pastry brush, lightly brush 14 by 9-inch rectangle in center of parchment with oil to cover area same size as phyllo. Lay 1 phyllo sheet on oiled parchment and brush thoroughly with oil. Repeat with 9 more phyllo sheets, brushing each with oil (you should have total of 10 layers of phyllo).

3  Spread spinach mixture evenly on phyllo, leaving ¼-inch border on all sides. Cover spinach with 6 more phyllo sheets, brushing each with oil and sprinkling each with about 2 tablespoons Pecorino. Lay 2 more phyllo sheets on top, brushing each with oil (these layers should not be sprinkled with Pecorino).

4  Working from center outward, use palms of your hands to compress layers and press out any air pockets. Using sharp knife, score spanakopita through top 3 layers of phyllo into 24 equal pieces. Sprinkle with sesame seeds (if using). Bake until phyllo is golden and crisp, 20 to 25 minutes. Let spanakopita cool on sheet for at least 10 minutes or up to 2 hours. Slide spanakopita, still on parchment, to cutting board. Cut into squares and serve.

# tomato and mozzarella tart

serves 6 to 8

2 (9½ by 9-inch) sheets puff pastry, thawed

1 large egg, lightly beaten

2 ounces Parmesan cheese, grated (1 cup)

1 pound plum tomatoes, cored and cut crosswise into ¼-inch-thick slices

Salt and pepper

2 tablespoons extra-virgin olive oil

2 garlic cloves, minced

8 ounces whole-milk mozzarella cheese, shredded (2 cups)

2 tablespoons chopped fresh basil

"
I love growing plum tomatoes to turn into homemade sauce. San Marzano tomatoes never fail, and I also like Amish Paste tomatoes. But for those times in high summer when the tomatoes are just perfect, I like to make this tart. It's simple yet stunning, and the layer of baked Parmesan that lies beneath the shingled, salted tomatoes adds just the right boost of seasoning. Fresh sliced or torn basil is perfect to use, but you can be adventurous and try other herbs like fresh thyme, oregano, sage, or even mint. "

*bridget*

1  Adjust oven rack to lower-middle position and heat oven to 425 degrees. Line rimmed baking sheet with parchment paper. Dust counter with flour and unfold both pieces of puff pastry onto counter. Brush 1 short edge of 1 sheet of pastry with egg and overlap with second sheet by 1 inch, forming 18 by 9-inch rectangle. Press to seal edges, then use rolling pin to smooth seam. Cut two 1-inch-wide strips from long side of dough and two more from short side. Transfer large piece of dough to prepared baking sheet and brush with egg. Attach long dough strips to long edges of dough and short strips to short edges, then brush dough strips with egg. Sprinkle Parmesan evenly over shell. Using fork, poke evenly spaced holes in surface of shell. Bake for 13 to 15 minutes, then reduce oven temperature to 350 degrees. Continue to bake until golden brown and crisp, 13 to 15 minutes longer. Transfer to wire rack; increase oven temperature to 425 degrees.

2  While shell bakes, place tomato slices in single layer on double layer of paper towels and sprinkle evenly with ½ teaspoon salt; let stand for 30 minutes. Place another double layer of paper towels on top of tomatoes and press firmly to dry tomatoes. Combine oil, garlic, and pinch each salt and pepper in small bowl; set aside.

3  Sprinkle mozzarella evenly over baked shell. Shingle tomato slices widthwise on top of cheese (about 4 slices per row); brush tomatoes with garlic oil. Bake until shell is deep golden brown and cheese is melted, 15 to 17 minutes. Let cool on wire rack for 5 minutes. Sprinkle with basil, slide onto cutting board or serving platter, cut into pieces, and serve.

# korean fried chicken wings

serves 4 to 6 as a main dish

1 tablespoon toasted sesame oil

1 teaspoon garlic, minced to paste

1 teaspoon grated fresh ginger

1¾ cups water

3 tablespoons sugar

2-3 tablespoons gochujang

1 tablespoon soy sauce

2 quarts vegetable oil

1 cup all-purpose flour

3 tablespoons cornstarch

3 pounds chicken wings, cut at joints, wingtips discarded

1  Combine sesame oil, garlic, and ginger in large bowl and microwave until mixture is bubbly and garlic and ginger are fragrant but not browned, 40 to 60 seconds. Whisk in ¼ cup water, sugar, gochujang, and soy sauce until smooth; set aside.

2  Add oil to large Dutch oven until it measures about 1½ inches deep and heat over medium-high heat to 350 degrees. While oil heats, whisk flour, cornstarch, and remaining 1½ cups water in second large bowl until smooth. Set wire rack in rimmed baking sheet and set aside.

3  Place half of wings in batter and stir to coat. Using tongs, remove wings from batter one at a time, allowing any excess batter to drip back into bowl, and add to hot oil. Increase heat to high and cook, stirring occasionally to prevent wings from sticking, until coating is light golden and beginning to crisp, about 7 minutes. (Oil temperature will drop sharply after adding wings.) Transfer wings to prepared rack. Return oil to 350 degrees and repeat with remaining wings. Reduce heat to medium and let second batch of wings rest for 5 minutes.

4  Heat oil to 375 degrees. Carefully return all wings to oil and cook, stirring occasionally, until deep golden brown and very crispy, about 7 minutes. Return wings to rack and let stand for 2 minutes. Transfer wings to reserved sauce and toss until coated. Return wings to rack and let stand for 2 minutes to allow coating to set. Transfer to platter and serve.

# batter fried chicken

serves 4 to 6

Salt

½ cup sugar

4 pounds bone-in chicken pieces (split breasts cut in half crosswise, drumsticks, and/or thighs), trimmed

1 cup all-purpose flour

1 cup cornstarch

5 teaspoons pepper

2 teaspoons baking powder

1 teaspoon paprika

½ teaspoon cayenne pepper

3 quarts peanut or vegetable oil

> Serving fried chicken to company would probably be considered an insult in many parts of the country, but not at my house. For me, fried chicken is a special event. And of all the recipes for fried chicken that I've tasted in the test kitchen over the years–and I've tasted dozens of batches of fried chicken–this is the recipe that I make at home. I love its light, crisp coating and am amazed at how well it reheats. Once fried, the chicken can be refrigerated and then reheated later in a hot oven with no effect on the texture of the coating– it's downright amazing. Brining the chicken before dipping it in the batter is crucial for keeping the chicken moist and juicy during frying and reheating.
>
> *julia*

1 Dissolve ½ cup salt and sugar in 2 quarts cold water in large container. Add chicken, cover, and refrigerate for 30 minutes to 1 hour.

2 Whisk flour, cornstarch, pepper, baking powder, paprika, cayenne, and 1 teaspoon salt together in large bowl. Whisk in 1¾ cups cold water until smooth; refrigerate until needed.

3 Add oil to large Dutch oven until it measures about 2 inches deep and heat over medium-high heat to 350 degrees. Remove chicken from brine and pat dry with paper towels. Remove batter from refrigerator and whisk to recombine. Set wire rack in rimmed baking sheet.

4 Add half of chicken to batter and coat thoroughly. Transfer chicken to hot oil, letting excess batter drip back into bowl. Fry chicken, adjusting burner as needed to maintain oil temperature between 300 and 325 degrees, until deep golden brown, breasts register 160 degrees, and thighs/drumsticks register 175 degrees, 12 to 15 minutes.

5 Transfer fried chicken to prepared wire rack and let drain. Return oil to 350 degrees and repeat with remaining chicken. Serve. (Fried chicken can be refrigerated for up to 1 day; reheat on wire rack in 400-degree oven for 10 to 15 minutes.)

# honey fried chicken

serves 4

### brine and chicken

½ cup salt

½ cup sugar

3 pounds bone-in chicken pieces (split breasts cut in half crosswise, drumsticks, and/or thighs), trimmed

### batter

1½ cups cornstarch

¾ cup cold water

2 teaspoons pepper

1 teaspoon salt

3 quarts peanut or vegetable oil

### honey glaze

¾ cup honey

2 tablespoons hot sauce

> The most dangerous place in the kitchen is the space between me and a platter of fried chicken. I will knock you down to get my hands on a just-fried drumstick or wing! But this isn't just any old fried chicken recipe. Oh no…this one sports a light-as-air, crisp shell that's great enough on its own. Of course, a final dip in a mix of honey and hot sauce makes this fried chicken so good, you'll thank your mama for bringing you into this world. 🙶
>
> *bridget*

1 **For the brine and chicken** Dissolve salt and sugar in 2 quarts cold water in large container. Submerge chicken in brine, cover, and refrigerate for 30 minutes to 1 hour.

2 **For the batter** While chicken is brining, whisk 1 cup cornstarch, water, pepper, and salt in large bowl until smooth. Refrigerate batter.

3 Set wire rack in rimmed baking sheet. Sift remaining ½ cup cornstarch into shallow bowl. Remove chicken from brine and dry thoroughly with paper towels. Working with 1 piece at a time, coat chicken thoroughly with cornstarch, shaking to remove excess; transfer to platter.

4 Add oil to large Dutch oven until it measures about 2 inches deep and heat over medium-high heat to 350 degrees. Whisk batter to recombine. Using tongs, transfer half of chicken to batter and turn to coat. Remove chicken from batter, 1 piece at a time, allowing excess to drip back into bowl, and transfer to hot oil. Fry chicken, stirring to prevent pieces from sticking together, until slightly golden and just beginning to crisp, 5 to 7 minutes. Adjust burner, if necessary, to maintain oil temperature between 325 and 350 degrees. (Chicken will not be cooked through at this point.) Transfer parcooked chicken to platter. Return oil to 350 degrees and repeat with remaining raw chicken and batter. Let each batch of chicken rest for 5 to 7 minutes.

5 Return oil to 350 degrees. Return first batch of chicken to oil and fry until breasts register 160 degrees and thighs/drumsticks register 175 degrees, 5 to 7 minutes. Transfer to prepared baking sheet. Return oil to 350 degrees and repeat with remaining chicken.

6 **For the honey glaze** Combine honey and hot sauce in large bowl and microwave until hot, about 1½ minutes. Add chicken pieces to honey mixture, one at a time, and turn to coat. Return to baking sheet, skin side up, to drain. Serve.

# za'atar butterflied chicken

serves 4

2 tablespoons za'atar

5 tablespoons plus 1 teaspoon extra-virgin olive oil

1 (3½- to 4-pound) whole chicken, giblets discarded

Salt and pepper

1 tablespoon minced fresh mint

¼ preserved lemon, pulp and white pith removed, rind rinsed and minced (1 tablespoon)

2 teaspoons white wine vinegar

½ teaspoon Dijon mustard

**"** Adding a simple paste of *za'atar* and olive oil to this easy roast chicken ratchets up the sophistication level a few notches for a nice midweek meal. Za'atar is the Arabic name for wild thyme but now commonly denotes an addictive spice mixture of thyme, sumac, and sesame. And rather than just rub it onto a plain roast chicken, I love how this recipe brushes it into a butterflied roast that has been browned in a skillet on the stovetop, so that the skin has a chance to render and get crisp first. The vinaigrette made with preserved lemons is amazing, but I sometimes substitute regular lemon zest or orange zest if I don't have any preserved lemons on hand. **"**

*julia*

1  Adjust oven rack to lowest position and heat oven to 450 degrees. Combine za'atar and 2 tablespoons oil in small bowl. With chicken breast side down, use kitchen shears to cut through bones on either side of backbone. Discard backbone and trim away excess fat and skin around neck. Flip chicken and tuck wingtips behind back. Press firmly on breastbone to flatten, then pound breast to be same thickness as legs and thighs. Pat chicken dry with paper towels and season with salt and pepper.

2  Heat 1 teaspoon oil in 12-inch ovensafe skillet over medium-high heat until just smoking. Place chicken skin side down in skillet, reduce heat to medium, and place heavy pot on chicken to press it flat. Cook chicken until skin is crisp and browned, about 25 minutes. (If chicken is not crisp after 20 minutes, increase heat to medium-high.)

3  Off heat, remove pot and carefully flip chicken. Brush skin with za'atar mixture, transfer skillet to oven, and roast until breast registers 160 degrees and thighs register 175 degrees, 10 to 20 minutes.

4  Transfer chicken to carving board and let rest for 10 minutes. Meanwhile, whisk mint, preserved lemon, vinegar, mustard, ⅛ teaspoon salt, and ⅛ teaspoon pepper in bowl until combined. Whisking constantly, slowly drizzle in remaining 3 tablespoons oil until emulsified. Carve chicken and serve with dressing.

# paella on the grill

serves 8

"

Each season during the filming of *ATK*, there's always one dish that stands out to me. It's one that I usually make on an episode, and I begin to make it at home…a lot. This grilled paella is everything you could want. Tender shrimp, juicy chicken, spices, and of course, that crisp, browned rice crust–*socarrat*–that forms on the bottom of the pan. Though there are quite a few parts to this recipe, it's deceptively simple to make, and your guests will be speechless. "

*bridget*

1½ pounds boneless, skinless chicken thighs, trimmed and halved crosswise

Salt and pepper

12 ounces jumbo shrimp (16 to 20 per pound), peeled and deveined

6 tablespoons extra-virgin olive oil

6 garlic cloves, minced

1¾ teaspoons smoked hot paprika

3 tablespoons tomato paste

4 cups chicken broth

1 (8-ounce) bottle clam juice

⅔ cup dry sherry

Pinch saffron threads, crumbled (optional)

1 onion, chopped fine

½ cup jarred roasted red peppers, chopped fine

3 cups Arborio rice

1 pound littleneck clams, scrubbed

1 pound Spanish-style chorizo sausage, cut into ½-inch pieces

1 cup frozen peas, thawed

Lemon wedges

1  Place chicken on large plate and sprinkle both sides with 1 teaspoon salt and 1 teaspoon pepper. Toss shrimp with 1 tablespoon oil, ½ teaspoon garlic, ¼ teaspoon paprika, and ¼ teaspoon salt in bowl until evenly coated. Set aside.

2  Heat 1 tablespoon oil in medium saucepan over medium heat until shimmering. Add remaining garlic and cook, stirring constantly, until garlic sticks to bottom of saucepan and begins to brown, about 1 minute. Add tomato paste and remaining 1½ teaspoons paprika and continue to cook, stirring constantly, until dark brown bits form on bottom of saucepan, about 1 minute. Add broth, clam juice, sherry, and saffron, if using. Increase heat to high and bring to boil. Remove saucepan from heat and set aside.

3A  For a charcoal grill  Open bottom vent completely. Light large chimney starter mounded with charcoal briquettes (7 quarts). When top coals are partially covered with ash, pour evenly over grill. Using tongs, arrange 20 unlit briquettes evenly over coals. Set cooking grate in place, cover, and open lid vent completely. Heat grill until hot, about 5 minutes.

3B  For a gas grill  Turn all burners to high, cover, and heat grill until hot, about 15 minutes. Leave all burners on high.

4  Clean and oil cooking grate. Place chicken on grill and cook until both sides are lightly browned, 5 to 7 minutes total. Return chicken to plate. Clean cooking grate.

5  Place roasting pan on grill (turning burners to medium-high if using gas) and add remaining ¼ cup oil. When oil begins to shimmer, add onion, red peppers, and ½ teaspoon salt. Cook, stirring frequently, until onion begins to brown, 4 to

7 minutes. Add rice (turning burners to medium if using gas) and stir until grains are well coated with oil.

6 Arrange chicken around perimeter of pan. Pour broth mixture and any accumulated juices from chicken over rice. Smooth rice into even layer, making sure nothing sticks to sides of pan and no rice rests atop chicken. When liquid reaches gentle simmer, place shrimp in center of pan in single layer. Arrange clams in center of pan, evenly distributing with shrimp and pushing hinge sides of clams into rice slightly so they stand up. Distribute chorizo evenly over surface of rice. Cook (covered if using gas), moving and rotating pan to maintain gentle simmer across entire surface of pan, until rice is almost cooked through, 12 to 18 minutes. (If using gas, heat can also be adjusted to maintain simmer.)

7 Sprinkle peas evenly over paella, cover grill, and cook until liquid is fully absorbed and rice on bottom of pan sizzles, 5 to 8 minutes. Continue to cook, uncovered, checking bottom of pan frequently with metal spoon, until uniform golden-brown crust forms, 8 to 15 minutes longer. (Rotate and slide pan around grill as necessary to ensure even crust formation.) Remove pan from grill, cover with aluminum foil, and let stand for 10 minutes. Serve with lemon wedges.

# the best sangria

serves 4

2 oranges (1 sliced, 1 juiced to yield ½ cup)

1 lemon, sliced

¼ cup superfine sugar

1 (750-ml) bottle fruity red wine, chilled

¼ cup triple sec

6-8 ice cubes

1  Add sliced orange, lemon, and sugar to large pitcher. Mash fruit gently with wooden spoon until fruit releases some juice, but is not totally crushed, and sugar dissolves, about 1 minute. Stir in orange juice, wine, and triple sec; refrigerate for at least 2 hours or up to 8 hours.

2  Before serving, add ice cubes and stir briskly to distribute settled fruit and pulp; serve immediately.

"

If you're making an amazing grilled paella for guests (page 174), do yourself a favor and whip up a batch of this sangria. I love this version because it doesn't require every fruit under the sun–just a couple of oranges and a lemon. In addition to the ice cubes called for in the recipe, I like to make a double batch of sangria and freeze some of it in ice cube trays. That way, you can serve up large goblets of the cocktail on the hottest of days, and if necessary, chill down the drinks without diluting them. "

*bridget*

# spanish grilled octopus salad with orange and bell pepper

serves 4 to 6

"

Grilled octopus is one of my all-time favorite foods and I never tire of eating it. Making it, however, can be tricky because the octopus needs to be double-cooked or it tastes like rubber. First, the octopus is simmered in a wine-based court bouillon (court bouillon is just a culinary school word for 'flavorful cooking liquid'), and then it gets grilled until the exterior is crisp before finally being tossed into a salad. The first chef who taught me how to cook octopus told me to add the corks from the wine bottles to the court bouillon to help tenderize the meat–although I know it's not true, I still sometimes add them for fun. Octopus can be found cleaned and frozen in the seafood section of specialty grocery stores and Asian markets. Be sure to rinse the defrosted octopus well, as sand can collect in the suckers. The octopus's membrane-like skin is easiest to peel while still warm, so be sure to do so as soon as it's cool enough to handle. "

*julia*

1 (4-pound) octopus, rinsed

2 cups dry white wine

6 garlic cloves (4 peeled and smashed, 2 minced)

2 bay leaves

7 tablespoons extra-virgin olive oil

1 teaspoon grated lemon zest plus ⅓ cup juice (2 lemons)

3 tablespoons sherry vinegar

2 teaspoons smoked paprika

1 teaspoon sugar

Salt and pepper

1 large orange

2 celery ribs, sliced thin on bias

1 red bell pepper, stemmed, seeded, and cut into 2-inch-long matchsticks

½ cup pitted brine-cured green olives, halved

2 tablespoons chopped fresh parsley

1  Using sharp knife, separate octopus mantle (large sac) and body (lower section with tentacles) from head (midsection containing eyes); discard head. Place octopus, wine, smashed garlic, and bay leaves in large pot, add water to cover octopus by 2 inches, and bring to simmer over high heat. Reduce heat to low, cover, and simmer gently, flipping octopus occasionally, until skin between tentacle joints tears easily when pulled, 45 minutes to 1¼ hours.

2  Transfer octopus to cutting board and let cool slightly; discard cooking liquid. Using paring knife, cut mantle in half, then trim and scrape away skin and interior fibers; transfer to bowl. Using your fingers, remove skin from body, being careful not to remove suction cups from tentacles. Cut tentacles from around core of body in 3 sections; discard core. Separate tentacles and transfer to bowl.

3  Whisk 6 tablespoons oil, lemon zest and juice, vinegar, paprika, sugar, ¼ teaspoon salt, ¼ teaspoon pepper, and minced garlic together in bowl; transfer to 1-gallon zipper-lock bag and set aside.

4A  For a charcoal grill  Open bottom vent completely. Light large chimney starter filled with charcoal briquettes (6 quarts). When top coals are partially covered with ash, pour evenly over half of grill. Set cooking grate in place, cover, and open lid vent completely. Heat grill until hot, about 5 minutes.

4B  For a gas grill  Turn all burners to high, cover, and heat grill until hot, about 15 minutes. Leave all burners on high.

5  Toss octopus with remaining 1 tablespoon oil. Clean cooking grate, then repeatedly brush grate with well-oiled paper towels until black and glossy, 5 to 10 times. Place

octopus on grill (directly over coals if using charcoal). Cook (covered if using gas) until octopus is streaked with dark grill marks and lightly charred at tips of tentacles, 8 to 10 minutes, flipping halfway through grilling; transfer to cutting board.

6 While octopus is still warm, slice ¼ inch thick on bias, then transfer to zipper-lock bag with oil-lemon mixture and toss to coat. Press out as much air from bag as possible and seal bag. Refrigerate for at least 2 hours or up to 24 hours, flipping bag occasionally.

7 Transfer octopus and marinade to large bowl and let come to room temperature, about 2 hours. Cut away peel and pith from orange. Holding fruit over bowl with octopus, use paring knife to slice between membranes to release segments. Add celery, bell pepper, olives, and parsley and gently toss to coat. Season with salt and pepper to taste. Serve.

*variation*
### greek grilled octopus salad with celery and fennel

Omit orange. Substitute 1 tablespoon dried oregano for paprika, 1 fennel bulb, stalks discarded, bulb halved, cored, and sliced thin, for bell pepper, and 2 tablespoons chopped fresh dill for parsley.

# grill-smoked salmon

serves 6

2 tablespoons sugar

1 tablespoon kosher salt

6 (6- to 8-ounce) center-cut skin-on salmon fillets

2 cups wood chips, 1 cup soaked in water for 15 minutes and drained

"

I'll never forget the first time I tried this salmon–it's a game changer. The salmon takes on a lovely, but not over-powering, smoky flavor and cooking it is a breeze because it's cooked on top of a piece of foil on the grill. I have a gas grill that I use for simple weeknight dinners, but I pull out the charcoal grill for this recipe–the smoky flavor comes through better with charcoal. Refrigerating the fish for an hour before cooking is crucial, as it gives the fish time to absorb the salt and sugar, and form a pellicle that helps the smoke absorb during cooking. I like using fruitwood chunks (such as apple and peach) for this; I'd stay away from mesquite because its flavor will be too strong. "

*julia*

1 Combine sugar and salt in bowl. Set salmon, skin side down, on wire rack set in rimmed baking sheet and sprinkle flesh side evenly with sugar mixture. Refrigerate, uncovered, for 1 hour. Meanwhile, using large piece of heavy-duty aluminum foil, wrap both soaked wood chips and remaining 1 cup unsoaked chips in 8 by 4½-inch foil packet. (Make sure chips do not poke holes in sides or bottom of packet.) Cut 2 evenly spaced 2-inch slits in top of packet.

2 Brush any excess salt and sugar from salmon using paper towels and blot salmon dry. Return fish to wire rack and refrigerate, uncovered, until ready to cook. Fold piece of heavy-duty foil into 18 by 6-inch rectangle.

3A For a charcoal grill Open bottom vent halfway. Light large chimney starter one-third filled with charcoal briquettes (2 quarts). When top coals are partially covered with ash, pour into steeply banked pile against side of grill. Place wood chip packet on coals. Set cooking grate in place, cover, and open lid vent half-way. Heat grill until hot and wood chips are smoking, about 5 minutes.

3B For a gas grill Remove cooking grate and place wood chip packet directly on primary burner. Set cooking grate in place and turn primary burner to high (leave other burner[s] off). Cover and heat grill until hot and wood chips begin to smoke, 15 to 25 minutes. Turn primary burner to medium. (Adjust primary burner as needed to maintain grill temperature between 275 to 300 degrees.)

4 Clean and oil cooking grate. Place foil rectangle on cooler side of grill and place salmon fillets on foil, spaced at least ½ inch apart. Cover (position lid vent over fish if using charcoal) and cook until center of salmon is still translucent when checked with tip of paring knife and registers 125 degrees (for medium-rare), 30 to 40 minutes. Transfer to platter. Serve warm or at room temperature.

# cod baked in foil with leeks and carrots

serves 4

4 tablespoons unsalted butter, softened

2 garlic cloves, minced

1¼ teaspoons finely grated lemon zest, plus lemon wedges for serving

1 teaspoon minced fresh thyme

Salt and pepper

2 tablespoons minced fresh parsley

2 leeks, white and light green parts only, cut into 2-inch-long segments, halved lengthwise, washed thoroughly, and cut into ⅛-inch-thick matchsticks

2 carrots, peeled and cut into 2-inch-long matchsticks

¼ cup dry vermouth or dry white wine

4 (6-ounce) skinless cod fillets, 1 to 1¼ inches thick

> Those of us who survived the food trends of the '80s will remember haute cuisine (those tiny portions!), flambéed desserts, and *cuisine en papillote*, or cooking in parchment. This dish is a take on the latter, with easy-to-crimp aluminum foil taking the place of frustrating-to-fold parchment. No matter the wrapper, the delicate fish inside comes out perfect each time, and the juices from the fish, vegetables, and vermouth turn into the most delicious broth. Best of all, it's perfect for entertaining, as the packets can be made well in advance, and the recipe doubles beautifully.
>
> *bridget*

1  Combine butter, 1 teaspoon garlic, ¼ teaspoon lemon zest, thyme, ¼ teaspoon salt, and ⅛ teaspoon pepper in small bowl. Combine parsley, remaining garlic, and remaining 1 teaspoon lemon zest in second small bowl and set aside. Place leeks and carrots in medium bowl, season with salt and pepper, and toss to combine.

2  Adjust oven rack to lower-middle position and heat oven to 450 degrees. Cut eight 12 by 12-inch sheets of aluminum foil; arrange 4 foil sheets flat on counter. Divide leek-carrot mixture among arranged foil sheets, mounding vegetables in center of each sheet. Pour 1 tablespoon vermouth over each mound of vegetables. Pat cod dry with paper towels, season with salt and pepper, and place 1 fillet on top of each vegetable mound. Divide butter mixture among fillets, spreading over top of each fillet. Place second foil sheet on top of cod, crimp edges together in ½-inch fold, then fold over 3 more times to create packet about 7 inches square. Place packets on rimmed baking sheet, overlapping slightly if necessary. (Packets can be refrigerated for up to 6 hours before baking. If packets are refrigerated for more than 30 minutes, increase cooking time by 2 minutes.)

3  Bake packets for 15 minutes, then transfer to individual plates. Open carefully (steam will escape) and, using metal spatula, gently slide contents onto plates, along with any accumulated juices. Sprinkle with parsley mixture. Serve immediately, passing lemon wedges separately.

# grilled shrimp skewers with lemon-garlic sauce

serves 8

4 pounds extra-large shrimp (21 to 25 per pound), peeled and deveined

¼ cup olive oil

Salt and pepper

¾ teaspoon sugar

12 tablespoons unsalted butter, cut into 12 pieces

⅓ cup lemon juice (2 lemons), plus lemon wedges for serving

5 garlic cloves, minced

¼ teaspoon red pepper flakes

⅓ cup minced fresh parsley

**"** I didn't think I could learn anything new about grilling shrimp until this recipe came along, which tosses the cooked shrimp in a lovely lemon-butter sauce right at the grill. It is simply the best grilled shrimp I've ever tasted and folks go nuts for it when I make it for a party. Given the simplicity of the recipe, it's no surprise that its success depends on using high-quality shrimp and butter. Be sure to buy shrimp that doesn't contain any chemicals; look at the label if it's frozen or ask the person behind the fish counter for more information. As for the butter, make sure it's fresh and unsalted; I love using Plugra European-Style Butter for this recipe. **"**

*julia*

1  Pat shrimp dry with paper towels. Thread shrimp tightly onto 8 metal skewers, alternating direction of heads and tails. Brush shrimp with oil and season with salt and pepper. Sprinkle one side of each skewer with sugar.

2  Cook butter, lemon juice, garlic, pepper flakes, and ¼ teaspoon salt together in small saucepan over medium heat, stirring often, until butter melts, about 2 minutes. Remove from heat and cover to keep warm.

3A  **For a charcoal grill**  Open bottom grill vent completely. Light large chimney starter mounded with charcoal briquettes (7 quarts). When top coals are partially covered with ash, pour evenly over grill. Set cooking grate in place, cover, and open lid vent completely. Heat grill until hot, about 5 minutes.

3B  **For a gas grill**  Turn all burners to high, cover, and heat grill until hot, about 15 minutes. Leave all burners on high.

4  Clean and oil cooking grate. Place shrimp skewers, sugared side down, on grill. Use tongs to push shrimp together on skewer if they have separated. Grill (covered if using gas) until shrimp are lightly charred, 4 to 5 minutes. Flip shrimp skewers and continue to grill (covered if using gas) until second side is pink, about 2 minutes longer.

5  Remove skewers from grill and gently slide shrimp off skewers into large, warmed bowl. Toss shrimp with warm butter sauce and parsley. Serve immediately with lemon wedges.

# grilled rack of lamb

serves 4 to 6

After a long New England winter, everyone is pretty excited to see the first signs of spring. The last of the snow piles melt away, the crocuses in our front yard pop up to say hi, and my grill, which I use occasionally during the winter, is almost in constant use. To celebrate spring, nothing beats a couple of racks of juicy, tender lamb, charred just enough on the grill. Most folks serve these on the bone, but since I am a devious soul, I remove the meat from the ribs so that I can have all those lamb bones to myself. "

*bridget*

4 teaspoons vegetable oil

4 teaspoons minced fresh rosemary

2 teaspoons minced fresh thyme

2 garlic cloves, minced

2 (1½- to 1¾-pound) racks of lamb (8 ribs each), trimmed and frenched

Salt and pepper

1 (13 by 9-inch) disposable aluminum roasting pan (if using charcoal)

1  Combine 1 tablespoon oil, rosemary, thyme, and garlic in bowl; set aside. Pat lamb dry with paper towels, rub with remaining 1 teaspoon oil, and season with salt and pepper.

2A  **For a charcoal grill**  Open bottom vent completely and place disposable pan in center of grill. Light large chimney starter filled with charcoal briquettes (6 quarts). When top coals are partially covered with ash, pour into 2 even piles on either side of disposable pan. Set cooking grate in place, cover, and open lid vent completely. Heat grill until hot, about 5 minutes.

2B  **For a gas grill**  Turn all burners to high, cover, and heat grill until hot, about 15 minutes. Leave primary burner on high and turn off other burner(s).

3  Clean and oil cooking grate. Place lamb, bone side up, on cooler part of grill with meaty side of racks very close to, but not quite over, hot coals or lit burner. Cover and cook until meat is lightly browned, faint grill marks appear, and fat has begun to render, 8 to 10 minutes.

4  Flip racks bone side down and slide to hotter part of grill. Cook until well browned, 3 to 4 minutes. Brush racks with herb mixture, flip bone side up, and cook until well browned, 3 to 4 minutes. Stand racks up, leaning them against each other for support, and cook until bottom is well browned and meat registers 120 to 125 degrees (for medium-rare) or 130 to 135 degrees (for medium), 3 to 8 minutes.

5  Transfer lamb to carving board, tent with aluminum foil, and let rest for 15 to 20 minutes. Cut between ribs to separate chops and serve.

# grilled lamb kofte

serves 4 to 6

"

I remember the first time I tasted these Middle Eastern kebabs in the test kitchen–I couldn't get enough of them. They have the most unusual balance of flavors that are familiar and comforting yet also somewhat sophisticated and luxurious–like a favorite, old white shirt that's been bleached and pressed so that it feels crisp and new again. I just love all the flavors–the lamb, the combination of hot and sweet spices, the fresh parsley and mint, and pine nuts and yogurt-tahini sauce. I usually make the skewers and then refrigerate them overnight so that they hold together better on the grill. I serve them with naan and steamed basmati rice, and I often double the amount of sauce because it tastes so darn good. "

*julia*

### yogurt-garlic sauce

1 cup plain whole-milk yogurt

2 tablespoons lemon juice

2 tablespoons tahini

1 garlic clove, minced

½ teaspoon salt

### kofte

½ cup pine nuts

4 garlic cloves, peeled

1½ teaspoons smoked hot paprika

1 teaspoon salt

1 teaspoon ground cumin

½ teaspoon pepper

¼ teaspoon ground coriander

¼ teaspoon ground cloves

⅛ teaspoon ground nutmeg

⅛ teaspoon ground cinnamon

1½ pounds ground lamb

½ cup grated onion, drained

⅓ cup minced fresh parsley

⅓ cup minced fresh mint

1½ teaspoons unflavored gelatin

1 (13 by 9-inch) disposable aluminum roasting pan (if using charcoal)

1  **For the yogurt-garlic sauce** Whisk all ingredients together in bowl.

2  **For the kofte** Process pine nuts, garlic, paprika, salt, cumin, pepper, coriander, cloves, nutmeg, and cinnamon into coarse paste in food processor, 30 to 45 seconds; transfer to large bowl. Add lamb, onion, parsley, mint, and gelatin to bowl and knead with your hands until thoroughly combined and mixture feels slightly sticky, about 2 minutes.

3  Divide mixture into 8 equal portions. Shape each portion into 5-inch-long cylinder about 1 inch in diameter. Using eight 12-inch metal skewers, thread 1 cylinder onto each skewer, pressing gently to adhere. Transfer skewers to lightly greased baking sheet, cover with plastic wrap, and refrigerate for 1 hour or up to 1 day.

4A  **For a charcoal grill** Using skewer, poke 12 holes in bottom of disposable pan. Open bottom vent completely and place disposable pan in center of grill. Light large chimney starter two-thirds filled with charcoal briquettes (4 quarts). When top coals are partially covered with ash, pour into disposable pan. Set cooking grate in place, cover, and open lid vent completely. Heat grill until hot, about 5 minutes.

4B  **For a gas grill** Turn all burners to high, cover, and heat grill until hot, about 15 minutes. Leave all burners on high.

5  Clean and oil cooking grate. Place skewers on grill (directly over coals if using charcoal) at 45-degree angle to bars. Cook (covered if using gas) until browned and meat easily releases from grill, 4 to 7 minutes. Flip skewers and continue to cook until browned on second side and meat registers 160 degrees, about 6 minutes. Transfer skewers to platter and serve, passing yogurt-garlic sauce separately.

# grilled citrus-marinated pork cutlets

serves 4 to 6

"

This little-known recipe from the ATK archives was developed for our *Best Mexican Recipes* cookbook, and I usually make it for friends at the cabin in the summertime. It's a casual meal, but it's a real looker once it has been plattered up, and the classic Mexican flavors of fresh lime, cilantro, radishes, and avocado taste great with ice-cold beer. Pounding the boneless country-style pork ribs into cutlets takes a little time, but it's not hard. Also, this recipe introduced me to annatto powder, which adds a cheery bright yellow-orange color and mild peppery-fruity flavor. (I thought I'd have a hard time finding annatto but found it easily in my favorite little supermarket down the street.) I usually serve this with tortillas that have been toasted on the grill, a simple cabbage-herb slaw, and a large tub of iced-down lawn mower beer (aka mild lager). "

*julia*

1½ pounds boneless country-style pork ribs, trimmed

⅓ cup lime juice (3 limes)

⅓ cup extra-virgin olive oil

3 garlic cloves, minced

1 tablespoon annatto powder

¾ teaspoon brown sugar

Salt and pepper

½ teaspoon ground coriander

1 (13 by 9-inch) disposable aluminum roasting pan (if using charcoal)

1 avocado, halved, pitted, and cut into ½-inch pieces

1 tomato, cored and cut into ½-inch pieces

2 radishes, trimmed and sliced thin

2 tablespoons chopped fresh cilantro

1  Cut each rib lengthwise to create 2 or 3 cutlets about ⅜ inch wide. Place cutlets cut side down between 2 sheets of plastic wrap and gently pound to even ¼-inch thickness.

2  Combine lime juice, oil, garlic, annatto powder, sugar, ¾ teaspoon salt, ½ teaspoon pepper, and coriander in 1-gallon zipper-lock bag. Add cutlets to bag and toss to coat. Press out as much air as possible, seal bag, and refrigerate for at least 30 minutes or up to 2 hours, flipping bag occasionally.

3  Just before grilling, remove cutlets from bag and pat dry with paper towels; discard marinade. If using charcoal, use kitchen shears to remove and discard bottom of disposable pan; reserve pan collar.

4A  For a charcoal grill  Open bottom vent completely. Light large chimney starter filled with charcoal briquettes (6 quarts). When top coals are partially covered with ash, place pan collar in center of grill, oriented over bottom vent, and pour coals into even layer in collar. Set cooking grate in place, cover, and open lid vent completely. Heat grill until hot, about 5 minutes.

4B  For a gas grill  Turn all burners to high, cover, and heat grill until hot, about 15 minutes. Leave all burners on high.

5  Clean and oil cooking grate. Place cutlets on grill (over coals if using charcoal). Cook, uncovered, until lightly browned on first side, about 2 minutes. Flip cutlets and continue to cook until just cooked through, about 30 seconds. Transfer cutlets to serving platter; top with avocado, tomato, radishes, and cilantro; and serve immediately.

# mexican street corn

serves 6

> These are great as a side dish, a snack, or as a fun party offering. After the corn is broiled, I like to cut the cobs into thirds, smother them with the tangy, salty mayo mixture, and serve them on wooden skewers so that guests can eat them neatly. I've also made them on the grill with great success. But I do like to add a pinch (or two) of cayenne pepper along with the chili powder. Corn *en fuego!*
>
> *bridget*

6 ears corn, husks and silk removed, stalks left intact

1 tablespoon olive oil

½ cup mayonnaise

1 ounce feta cheese, crumbled (¼ cup)

2 tablespoons minced fresh cilantro

1 tablespoon lime juice, plus lime wedges for serving

1 garlic clove, minced

1 teaspoon chili powder

Salt and pepper

1  Adjust oven rack 5 inches from broiler element and heat broiler. Line rimmed baking sheet with aluminum foil. Brush corn all over with oil and transfer to prepared sheet. Broil corn until well browned on 1 side, about 10 minutes. Flip corn and broil until browned on opposite side, about 10 minutes longer.

2  Meanwhile, whisk mayonnaise, feta, cilantro, lime juice, garlic, chili powder, and ¼ teaspoon salt in bowl until incorporated.

3  Remove corn from oven and brush evenly on all sides with mayonnaise mixture. (Reserve any extra mayonnaise mixture for serving.) Return corn to oven and broil, rotating frequently, until coating is lightly browned, about 2 minutes. Season with salt and pepper to taste. Serve corn with lime wedges and any extra mayonnaise mixture.

# wheat berry salad with blueberries and goat cheese

serves 4 to 6

"

Grain salads are my preferred lunch when I'm working and this is one of my all-time favorites. I'm usually not a big fan of fresh fruit in savory salads, but the blueberries and goat cheese are a terrific match with the earthy-tasting wheat berries here. Also, this recipe finally gave me a foolproof way to cook wheat berries, because they can be tough little suckers! I once had a pot of wheat berries cooking on the stove for nearly 2 hours and I just couldn't get them tender. The trick is to not use too much salt, because if the salinity in the cooking water is too high it will prevent the wheat berries from absorbing the water. I don't often measure the amount of salt I add to a large pot of boiling water, but I learned the hard way that measuring it is important when cooking wheat berries. Also, I've found that this salad holds well for several days, so it's perfect for casual parties. "

*julia*

1½ cups wheat berries

Salt and pepper

2 tablespoons champagne vinegar

1 tablespoon minced shallot

1 tablespoon minced fresh chives

1 teaspoon Dijon mustard

6 tablespoons extra-virgin olive oil

2 heads Belgian endive (4 ounces each), halved, cored, and sliced crosswise ¼ inch thick

7½ ounces (1½ cups) blueberries

¾ cup pecans, toasted and chopped coarse

4 ounces goat cheese, crumbled (1 cup)

1  Bring 4 quarts water to boil in large pot. Add wheat berries and ¼ teaspoon salt, partially cover, and cook, stirring often, until wheat berries are tender but still chewy, 50 minutes to 1 hour 10 minutes. Drain and rinse under cold running water until cool; drain well.

2  Whisk vinegar, shallot, chives, mustard, ½ teaspoon salt, and ¼ teaspoon pepper together in large bowl. Whisking constantly, drizzle in oil. Add wheat berries, endive, blueberries, and pecans and toss to combine. Season with salt and pepper to taste, sprinkle with goat cheese, and serve.

# tomato and burrata salad with pangrattato and basil

serves 4 to 6

‟

Tomato and fresh mozzarella salad has been my go-to offering for large potlucks and family get-togethers for years and I thought I had it pretty nailed down until this recipe came along–it's kicked my little salad off the menu forever. Burrata is a type of fresh mozzarella with a creamy, liquid center and it's pure heaven when its flavor mixes with all the tomato juice on the platter. Also, I think that chopping the tomatoes (rather than slicing them) and using a combination of regular and cherry tomatoes is pretty clever. Not only are the chopped tomatoes much easier to eat (especially at a potluck) but the combination of regular and cherry tomatoes gives the salad more variation in terms of flavors and textures. The thing that takes this salad over the top, however, are the garlicky bread crumbs that help soak up the all the juices. „

*julia*

1½ pounds very ripe tomatoes, cored and cut into 1-inch pieces

8 ounces ripe cherry tomatoes, halved

Salt and pepper

3 ounces rustic Italian bread, cut into 1-inch pieces (1 cup)

6 tablespoons extra-virgin olive oil

1 garlic clove, minced

1 shallot, halved and sliced thin

1½ tablespoons white balsamic vinegar

½ cup chopped fresh basil

8 ounces burrata cheese, room temperature

1  Toss tomatoes with ¼ teaspoon salt and let drain in colander for 30 minutes.

2  Pulse bread in food processor into large crumbs measuring between ⅛ and ¼ inch, about 10 pulses. Combine crumbs, 2 tablespoons oil, pinch salt, and pinch pepper in 12-inch nonstick skillet. Cook over medium heat, stirring often, until crumbs are crisp and golden, about 10 minutes. Clear center of skillet, add garlic, and cook, mashing it into skillet, until fragrant, about 30 seconds. Stir garlic into crumbs. Transfer to plate and let cool slightly.

3  Whisk shallot, vinegar, and ¼ teaspoon salt together in large bowl. Whisking constantly, slowly drizzle in remaining ¼ cup oil. Add tomatoes and basil and gently toss to combine. Season with salt and pepper to taste, and arrange on serving platter. Cut burrata into 1-inch pieces, collecting creamy liquid. Sprinkle burrata over tomatoes and drizzle with creamy liquid. Sprinkle with bread crumbs and serve immediately.

# fusilli salad with salami, provolone, and sun-dried tomato vinaigrette

serves 8 to 10

I moved to San Francisco right out of culinary school. I lived on upper Page Street, near the park and Haight-Ashbury, where there was terrific, inexpensive food all around. One of my favorite spots, however, was Molinari Delicatessen down in North Beach–they made sandwiches and salads loaded with their own cured meats, cheese, and pickled vegetables. The flavors of this pasta salad with the salami, provolone, capers, and olives reminds me of those killer sandwiches and it has become a summer staple at my house when we have a party. Rinsing the pasta with cold water after cooking it and leaving it slightly wet ensures that the pasta will have a nice springy texture and the salad won't be dry. "

*julia*

Salt and pepper

1 pound fusilli

1 cup oil-packed sun-dried tomatoes, rinsed, patted dry, and minced

6 tablespoons extra-virgin olive oil

¼ cup red wine vinegar

2 tablespoons chopped fresh basil or parsley

1 garlic clove, minced

8 ounces thickly sliced salami or pepperoni, cut into matchsticks

8 ounces thickly sliced provolone, cut into matchsticks

1½ ounces (1½ cups) baby spinach

½ cup pitted kalamata olives, sliced

1 Bring 4 quarts water to boil in large pot. Add 1 tablespoon salt and pasta and cook, stirring often, until tender. Drain pasta, rinse with cold water, and drain again, leaving pasta slightly wet.

2 Meanwhile, whisk sun-dried tomatoes, oil, vinegar, basil, garlic, ½ teaspoon salt, and ½ teaspoon pepper together in large bowl.

3 Add pasta and salami to vinaigrette and toss to combine. Cover and let sit for 10 minutes. (Salad can be refrigerated in airtight container for up to 1 day; before continuing, add warm water and additional oil as needed to refresh.)

4 Before serving, stir in provolone, spinach, and olives and season with salt and pepper to taste.

# mushroom and leek galette

serves 6

### dough

1¼ cups (6¼ ounces) all-purpose flour

½ cup (2¾ ounces) whole-wheat flour

1 tablespoon sugar

¾ teaspoon salt

10 tablespoons unsalted butter, cut into ½-inch pieces and chilled

7 tablespoons ice water

1 teaspoon distilled white vinegar

### filling

1¼ pounds shiitake mushrooms, stemmed and sliced thin

5 teaspoons olive oil

1 pound leeks, white and light green parts only, halved lengthwise, sliced ½ inch thick, and washed thoroughly (3 cups)

1 teaspoon minced fresh thyme

2 tablespoons crème fraîche

1 tablespoon Dijon mustard

Salt and pepper

3 ounces Gorgonzola cheese, crumbled (¾ cup)

1 large egg, lightly beaten

Kosher salt

2 tablespoons minced fresh parsley

**1  For the dough**  Process all-purpose flour, whole-wheat flour, sugar, and salt in food processor until combined, about 5 seconds. Scatter butter over top and pulse until it forms pea-size pieces, about 10 pulses. Transfer mixture to medium bowl.

**2**  Sprinkle ice water and vinegar over mixture. With rubber spatula, use folding motion to mix until loose, shaggy mass forms with some dry flour remaining (do not overwork). Transfer mixture to large sheet of plastic wrap, press gently into rough 4-inch square, and wrap tightly. Refrigerate for 45 minutes.

**3**  Transfer dough to floured counter. Roll into 11 by 8-inch rectangle with short side parallel to edge of counter. Using bench scraper, bring bottom third of dough up, then fold upper third over it, folding like business letter into 8 by 4-inch rectangle. Turn dough 90 degrees counterclockwise. Roll dough again into 11 by 8-inch rectangle and fold into thirds again. Turn dough 90 degrees counterclockwise and repeat rolling and folding into thirds. After last fold, fold dough in half to create 4-inch square. Press top of dough to seal. Wrap in plastic and refrigerate for at least 45 minutes or up to 2 days.

**4  For the filling**  Microwave mushrooms, covered, until just tender, 3 to 5 minutes. Transfer to colander and let drain; return to bowl. Meanwhile, heat 1 tablespoon oil in 12-inch skillet over medium heat until shimmering. Add leeks and thyme, cover, and cook, stirring occasionally, until leeks are tender and beginning to brown, 5 to 7 minutes. Transfer to bowl with mushrooms. Stir in crème fraîche and mustard. Season with salt and pepper to taste; set aside.

**5** Adjust oven rack to lower-middle position, set baking stone on rack, and heat oven to 400 degrees. Line rimmed baking sheet with parchment paper. Remove dough from refrigerator and let stand at room temperature for 15 to 20 minutes. Roll dough into 14-inch circle about $\frac{1}{8}$ inch thick on floured counter. (Trim edges as needed to form rough circle.) Transfer dough to prepared sheet. Using straw or tip of paring knife, cut five $\frac{1}{4}$-inch circles in dough (one at center and four evenly spaced halfway from center to edge of dough). Brush top of dough with 1 teaspoon oil.

**6** Spread half of filling evenly over dough, leaving 2-inch border around edge. Sprinkle half of Gorgonzola over filling, cover with remaining filling, and top with remaining Gorgonzola. Drizzle remaining 1 teaspoon oil over filling. Grasp 1 edge of dough and fold outer 2 inches over filling. Repeat around circumference of tart, overlapping dough every 2 to 3 inches; gently pinch pleated dough to secure but do not press dough into filling. Brush dough with egg and sprinkle evenly with kosher salt.

**7** Lower oven temperature to 375 degrees. Set sheet on stone and bake until crust is deep golden brown and filling is beginning to brown, 35 to 45 minutes. Let tart cool on sheet on wire rack for 10 minutes. Using offset or wide metal spatula, loosen tart from parchment and carefully slide it onto cutting board. Sprinkle parsley over filling, cut into wedges, and serve.

# indian-style vegetable curry with potatoes and cauliflower

serves 4 to 6

1 (14.5-ounce) can diced tomatoes

3 tablespoons vegetable oil

4 teaspoons curry powder

1½ teaspoons garam masala

2 onions, chopped fine

12 ounces red potatoes, unpeeled, cut into ½-inch chunks

Salt and pepper

3 garlic cloves, minced

1 serrano chile, stemmed, seeded, and minced

1 tablespoon grated fresh ginger

1 tablespoon tomato paste

½ head cauliflower (1 pound), cored and cut into 1-inch florets

1½ cups water

1 (15-ounce) can chickpeas, rinsed

1½ cups frozen peas

½ cup canned coconut milk

¼ cup minced fresh cilantro

1 recipe Indian-Style Onion Relish (recipe follows)

1 recipe Cilantro-Mint Chutney (recipe follows)

"

For me, this vegetable curry is comfort food at its best. I make it about once a month for dinner, but also when family and friends are coming over. I like serving it for casual company because it's unexpected, it's healthy, and it has a wonderful deep, rich flavor. In fact, when a younger cousin in college asked me to help him learn how to cook a few things (and maybe impress a young lady), I taught him this recipe. Lots of fancy recipes for curry have you make a curry powder from scratch, which is great if you have time, but I'm fine using store-bought powder and gussying up the flavor with a little garam masala. And although the ingredient list for this recipe is rather long, the cooking happens quickly. Be sure to make the relish and chutney to serve along-side the curry; they take the flavors over the top. Serve with basmati rice and naan. "

*julia*

1  Pulse diced tomatoes and their juice in food processor until nearly smooth, with some ¼-inch pieces visible, about 3 pulses.

2  Heat oil in Dutch oven over medium-high heat until shimmering. Add curry powder and garam masala and cook until fragrant, about 10 seconds. Stir in onions, potatoes, and ¼ teaspoon salt and cook, stirring occasionally, until onions are browned and potatoes are golden brown at edges, about 10 minutes.

3  Reduce heat to medium. Stir in garlic, serrano, ginger, and tomato paste and cook until fragrant, about 30 seconds. Add cauliflower florets and cook, stirring constantly, until florets are coated with spices, about 2 minutes.

4  Gradually stir in water, scraping up any browned bits. Stir in chickpeas and processed tomatoes and bring to simmer. Cover, reduce to gentle simmer, and cook until vegetables are tender, 20 to 25 minutes.

5  Uncover, stir in peas and coconut milk, and continue to cook until peas are heated through, 1 to 2 minutes. Off heat, stir in cilantro, season with salt and pepper to taste, and serve with Indian-Style Onion Relish and Cilantro-Mint Chutney.

### indian-style onion relish
makes about 1 cup

1 Vidalia onion, chopped fine

1 tablespoon lime juice

½ teaspoon paprika

½ teaspoon sugar

⅛ teaspoon salt

Pinch cayenne pepper

Mix all ingredients together in bowl. (Relish can be refrigerated for up to 1 day.)

### cilantro-mint chutney
makes about 1 cup

2 cups fresh cilantro leaves

1 cup fresh mint leaves

⅓ cup plain yogurt

¼ cup finely chopped onion

1 tablespoon lime juice

1½ teaspoons sugar

½ teaspoon ground cumin

¼ teaspoon salt

Process all ingredients in food processor until smooth, about 20 seconds, stopping to scrape down bowl as needed. (Chutney can be refrigerated for up to 1 day.)

# new mexican pork stew

serves 6 to 8

¾ ounce dried ancho chiles (about 3 chiles)

8 cups chicken broth

2 pounds boneless country-style pork ribs, trimmed

Salt and pepper

3 tablespoons vegetable oil

3 (15-ounce) cans white hominy, rinsed

2 onions, chopped

5 garlic cloves, minced

1 tablespoon minced fresh oregano

1 tablespoon lime juice

" The first time that I had posole (or pozole) was at a former coworker's wedding reception. Both sides of the wedding party catered the event, and since they were from Mexico, the food was as spectacular as it was varied. We dined on mole (yum) and menudo (still learning to love that one) but it was the posole that I remember the most. Flavored with pork broth and just enough chile heat to keep us celebrating through the night, it's a stew that's perfect for any occasion. "

*bridget*

1 Adjust oven rack to middle position and heat oven to 350 degrees. Place chiles on baking sheet and bake until puffed and fragrant, about 6 minutes. When chiles are cool enough to handle, remove stems and seeds. Combine chiles and 1 cup broth in medium bowl. Cover and microwave until bubbling, about 2 minutes. Let stand until softened, 10 to 15 minutes.

2 Pat pork dry with paper towels and season with salt and pepper. Heat 2 tablespoons oil in Dutch oven over medium-high heat until just smoking. Cook pork until well browned all over, about 10 minutes. Transfer pork to plate. Add hominy to now-empty pot and cook, stirring frequently, until fragrant and hominy begins to darken, 2 to 3 minutes. Transfer hominy to medium bowl.

3 Heat remaining 1 tablespoon oil in now-empty pot over medium heat until shimmering. Add onions and cook until softened, about 5 minutes. Stir in garlic and cook until fragrant, about 30 seconds. Puree onion mixture with softened chile mixture in blender. Combine remaining 7 cups broth, pureed onion-chile mixture, pork, oregano, ½ teaspoon salt, and ½ teaspoon pepper in now-empty pot and bring to boil. Reduce heat to low and simmer, covered, until meat is tender, 1 to 1½ hours.

4 Transfer pork to clean plate. Add hominy to pot and simmer, covered, until tender, about 30 minutes. Skim fat from broth. When meat is cool enough to handle, shred into bite-size pieces, discarding fat. Return pork to pot and cook until heated through, about 1 minute. Off heat, add lime juice. Season with salt and pepper to taste. Serve. (Posole can be refrigerated for up to 3 days.)

*Casual Entertaining*

# weeknight tagliatelle with bolognese sauce

serves 4 to 6

For years, Ian and I have been on a never-ending search for the best Bolognese sauce–either homemade or at a restaurant. We've ordered it all over town and tried a variety of recipes (including other ATK recipes), but none of them were 'our' Bolognese. We wanted the meat to be supertender and the sauce to have a rich meaty flavor, a slightly sweet finish, and solid tomato presence. Then we tried this new recipe from *Cook's Illustrated* and finally found what we were looking for. Surprisingly, it doesn't call for milk (it uses a big handful of Parmesan instead) and it adds reduced beef broth and some pancetta to bolster the meaty flavor–very clever. To ensure that the meat stays tender, it is tossed with baking soda before being added to the pot. Note that the finished sauce will look very thin, but resist the urge to reduce it further; the tagliatelle absorbs all the extra moisture when tossed with the sauce. If you can't find tagliatelle, you can substitute pappardelle. Substituting other pasta may result in a too-wet sauce. ❞

*julia*

1 pound 93 percent lean ground beef

¼ teaspoon baking soda

Salt and pepper

4 cups beef broth

6 ounces pancetta, chopped coarse

1 onion, chopped coarse

1 large carrot, peeled and chopped coarse

1 celery rib, chopped coarse

1 tablespoon unsalted butter

1 tablespoon extra-virgin olive oil

3 tablespoons tomato paste

1 cup dry red wine

1 ounce Parmesan cheese, grated (½ cup), plus extra for serving

1 pound tagliatelle

1  Toss beef with 2 tablespoons water, baking soda, and ¼ teaspoon pepper in bowl until thoroughly combined. Set aside.

2  While beef sits, bring broth to boil over high heat in large pot (this pot will be used to cook pasta in step 6) and cook until reduced to 2 cups, about 15 minutes; set aside.

3  Pulse pancetta in food processor until finely chopped, 15 to 20 pulses. Add onion, carrot, and celery and pulse until vegetables are finely chopped and mixture has paste-like consistency, 12 to 15 pulses, scraping down sides of bowl as needed.

4  Heat butter and oil in Dutch oven over medium-high heat until shimmering. Add pancetta-vegetable mixture and ¼ teaspoon pepper and cook, stirring occasionally, until liquid has evaporated, about 8 minutes. Spread mixture in even layer in bottom of pot and continue to cook, stirring every couple of minutes, until very dark browned bits form on bottom of pot, 7 to 12 minutes longer. Stir in tomato paste and cook until paste is rust-colored and bottom of pot is dark brown, 1 to 2 minutes.

5  Reduce heat to medium, add beef, and cook, using wooden spoon to break meat into pieces no larger than ¼ inch, until beef has just lost its raw pink color, 4 to 7 minutes. Stir in wine, scraping up any browned bits, and bring to simmer. Cook until wine has evaporated and sauce has thickened, about 5 minutes. Stir in broth and Parmesan. Return sauce to simmer; cover, reduce heat to low, and simmer for 30 minutes (sauce will look thin). Remove from heat and season with salt and pepper to taste.

6  While sauce simmers, bring 4 quarts water to boil in clean, dry pot. Add pasta and 1 tablespoon salt and cook, stirring occasionally, until al dente. Reserve ¼ cup cooking water, then drain pasta. Add pasta to pot with sauce and toss to combine. Adjust sauce consistency with reserved cooking water as needed. Transfer to platter or individual bowls and serve, passing extra Parmesan separately.

# catalan-style beef stew

serves 4 to 6

### stew

2 tablespoons olive oil

2 large onions, chopped fine

½ teaspoon sugar

Kosher salt and pepper

2 plum tomatoes, halved lengthwise, pulp grated on large holes of box grater, and skins discarded

1 teaspoon smoked paprika

1 bay leaf

1½ cups dry white wine

1½ cups water

1 large sprig fresh thyme

¼ teaspoon ground cinnamon

2½ pounds boneless beef short ribs, trimmed and cut into 2-inch cubes

### picada

¼ cup whole blanched almonds

2 tablespoons olive oil

1 slice hearty white sandwich bread, crust removed, torn into 1-inch pieces

2 garlic cloves, peeled

3 tablespoons minced fresh parsley

8 ounces oyster mushrooms, trimmed

1 teaspoon sherry vinegar

**1 For the stew** Adjust oven rack to middle position and heat oven to 300 degrees. Heat oil in Dutch oven over medium-low heat until shimmering. Add onions, sugar, and ½ teaspoon salt; cook, stirring often, until onions are deeply caramelized, 30 to 40 minutes. Add tomato pulp, paprika, and bay leaf; cook, stirring often, until darkened and thick, 5 to 10 minutes.

**2** Add wine, water, thyme sprig, and cinnamon to pot, scraping up any browned bits. Season short ribs with 1½ teaspoons salt and ½ teaspoon pepper and add to pot. Increase heat to high and bring to simmer. Transfer to oven and cook, uncovered. After 1 hour, stir stew to redistribute meat, return to oven, and continue to cook until meat is tender, 1½ to 2 hours longer.

**3 For the picada** While stew is in oven, heat almonds and 1 tablespoon oil in 10-inch skillet over medium heat; cook, stirring often, until almonds are golden brown, 3 to 6 minutes. Using slotted spoon, transfer almonds to food processor. Return now-empty skillet to medium heat, add bread, and cook, stirring often, until toasted, 2 to 4 minutes; transfer to food processor with almonds. Add garlic to almonds and bread and process until mixture is finely ground, about 20 seconds, scraping down bowl as needed. Transfer mixture to separate bowl, stir in parsley, and set aside.

**4** Return now-empty skillet to medium heat. Heat remaining 1 tablespoon oil until shimmering. Add mushrooms and ½ teaspoon salt; cook, stirring often, until tender, 5 to 7 minutes. Transfer to bowl and set aside.

**5** Discard bay leaf and thyme sprig. Stir picada, mushrooms, and vinegar into stew. Season with salt and pepper to taste, and serve.

# éclair cake

serves 15

I don't bake lots of cakes—in fact, I don't care much for traditional cakes at all—but this 'cake' is one of my all-time favorite guilty pleasures. Calling it a cake is a real stretch—it's more like a trifle made with homemade vanilla pudding, graham crackers, and a shiny chocolate ganache top. As the grahams and pudding sit overnight, the grahams absorb moisture and soften to a cake-like consistency while the pudding firms up to become sliceable. It's not a fancy or exotic dessert, but it's always a home run with kids and adults alike. Along with the Slow-Roasted Pork Shoulder with Peach Sauce (page 245), it has become a standard at our Davison family Christmas celebration. Although the cake is servable after sitting for 6 hours, its texture is much better (more sliceable) if you let it sit for 24 hours. ”

*julia*

1¼ cups (8¾ ounces) sugar

6 tablespoons (1½ ounces) cornstarch

1 teaspoon salt

5 cups whole milk

4 tablespoons unsalted butter, cut into 4 pieces

5 teaspoons vanilla extract

1¼ teaspoons unflavored gelatin

2 tablespoons water

2¾ cups heavy cream, chilled

14 ounces whole graham crackers

1 cup (6 ounces) semisweet chocolate chips

5 tablespoons light corn syrup

1 Combine sugar, cornstarch, and salt in large saucepan. Whisk milk into sugar mixture until smooth and bring to boil, scraping bottom of pan with heat-resistant rubber spatula, over medium-high heat. Immediately reduce heat to medium-low and cook, continuing to scrape bottom, until thickened and large bubbles appear on surface, 4 to 6 minutes. Off heat, whisk in butter and vanilla. Transfer pudding to large bowl and place plastic wrap directly on surface of pudding. Refrigerate until cool, about 2 hours.

2 Sprinkle gelatin over water in bowl and let sit until gelatin softens, about 5 minutes. Microwave until mixture is bubbling around edges and gelatin dissolves, 15 to 30 seconds. Using stand mixer fitted with whisk, whip 2 cups cream on medium-low speed until foamy, about 1 minute. Increase speed to high and whip until soft peaks form, 1 to 3 minutes. Add gelatin mixture and whip until stiff peaks form, about 1 minute.

3 Whisk one-third of whipped cream into chilled pudding, then gently fold in remaining whipped cream, 1 scoop at a time, until combined. Cover bottom of 13 by 9-inch baking dish with layer of graham crackers, breaking crackers as necessary to line bottom of pan. Top with half of pudding–whipped cream mixture (about 5 ½ cups) and another layer of graham crackers. Repeat with remaining pudding–whipped cream mixture and remaining graham crackers.

4 Microwave chocolate chips, remaining ¾ cup cream, and corn syrup in bowl, on 50 percent power, stirring occasionally, until smooth, 1 to 2 minutes. Let glaze cool to room temperature, about 10 minutes. Cover graham crackers with glaze and refrigerate cake for 6 to 24 hours. Serve. (Cake can be refrigerated for up to 2 days.)

# perfect latin flan

serves 8 to 10

⅔ cup (4⅔ ounces) sugar

2 large eggs plus 5 large yolks

1 (14-ounce) can sweetened condensed milk

1 (12-ounce) can evaporated milk

½ cup whole milk

1½ tablespoons vanilla extract

½ teaspoon salt

"
While I love a good crème caramel, I've always felt that dealing with lots of little ramekins is a bit fussy. Enter the flan. Baked in a good old loaf pan, it's easy to make, impressive to serve, and, thanks to both evaporated and sweetened condensed milk, it's more flavorful than a plain vanilla crème caramel. Custard. Caramel. Need I say more? "

*bridget*

1 Stir sugar and ¼ cup water in medium heavy saucepan until sugar is completely moistened. Bring to boil over medium-high heat, 3 to 5 minutes, and cook, without stirring, until mixture begins to turn golden, another 1 to 2 minutes. Gently swirling pan, continue to cook until sugar is color of peanut butter, 1 to 2 minutes. Remove from heat and swirl pan until sugar is reddish amber and fragrant, 15 to 20 seconds. Carefully swirl in 2 tablespoons warm tap water until incorporated; mixture will bubble and steam. Pour caramel into 8½ by 4½-inch loaf pan; do not scrape out saucepan. Set loaf pan aside.

2 Adjust oven rack to middle position and heat oven to 300 degrees. Line bottom of 13 by 9-inch baking pan with dish towel, folding towel to fit smoothly, and set aside. Bring 2 quarts water to boil.

3 Whisk eggs and yolks in large bowl until combined. Add condensed milk, evaporated milk, whole milk, vanilla, and salt and whisk until incorporated. Strain mixture through fine-mesh strainer into prepared loaf pan.

4 Cover loaf pan tightly with aluminum foil and place in prepared baking pan. Place baking pan in oven and carefully pour boiling water into pan. Bake until center of custard jiggles slightly when shaken and custard registers 180 degrees, 1¼ to 1½ hours. Remove foil and leave custard in water bath until loaf pan has cooled completely. Remove loaf pan from water bath, wrap tightly with plastic wrap, and chill overnight or up to 4 days.

5 To unmold, slide paring knife around edges of pan. Invert serving platter on top of pan and turn pan and platter over. When flan is released, remove loaf pan. Using rubber spatula, scrape residual caramel onto flan. Slice and serve. (Leftover flan can be refrigerated for up to 4 days.)

# dark chocolate cupcakes with vanilla frosting

makes 12 cupcakes

I make cupcakes once a year for my daughter's birthday parties at home and at school, and this is the recipe I use. I've tried to get away with boxed cake mixes but they never work right for me (they turn out with huge air pockets in the crumb) and they make me feel guilty. I mean, for goodness' sake, if there's one thing I should be able to find time to do, it's making homemade cupcakes for my daughter's birthday. I prefer this recipe because it's both delicious and easy–it doesn't even require pulling out a mixer or a food processor. Plus, the combination of cocoa powder and bittersweet chocolate gives the cake a deep, hearty chocolate flavor that's not too sweet. To top the cupcakes off, I always make a vanilla frosting with butter and powdered sugar to which I add food coloring for fun. Also, I like this frosting recipe because it makes plenty, so you can really pile it on top of the cupcakes. I usually have to make 24 cupcakes, but have found that this recipe doesn't double well; I just make two batches instead. ”

*julia*

8 tablespoons unsalted butter, cut into 4 pieces

2 ounces bittersweet chocolate, chopped

½ cup (1½ ounces) Dutch-processed cocoa powder

¾ cup (3¾ ounces) all-purpose flour

¾ teaspoon baking powder

½ teaspoon baking soda

2 large eggs

¾ cup (5¼ ounces) sugar

1 teaspoon vanilla extract

½ teaspoon salt

½ cup sour cream

1 recipe Vanilla Frosting (recipe follows)

1 Adjust oven rack to lower-middle position and heat oven to 350 degrees. Line 12-cup muffin tin with paper liners.

2 Combine butter, chocolate, and cocoa in medium heatproof bowl. Set bowl over saucepan filled with 1 inch of barely simmering water. Cook, stirring occasionally, until butter and chocolate are melted. Whisk until smooth and let cool slightly.

3 Whisk flour, baking powder, and baking soda together in bowl. In medium bowl, whisk eggs until combined, then whisk in sugar, vanilla, and salt until fully incorporated. Whisk in cooled chocolate mixture until combined. Sift about one-third of flour mixture over chocolate mixture and whisk until combined. Whisk in sour cream until combined. Sift remaining flour mixture over batter and whisk until batter is homogeneous and thick.

4 Divide batter evenly among muffin cups. Bake cupcakes until toothpick inserted into center comes out with few crumbs attached, 18 to 20 minutes, rotating muffin tin halfway through baking. Let cupcakes cool in muffin tin for 15 minutes, then carefully transfer to wire rack and let cool to room temperature, about 30 minutes.

5 Mound frosting in center of each cupcake. Using small icing spatula or butter knife, spread icing to edge of cupcake, leaving slight mound in center. Serve.

## vanilla frosting

makes about 3 cups

20 tablespoons (2½ sticks) unsalted butter, cut into chunks and softened

2 tablespoons heavy cream

2 teaspoons vanilla extract

⅛ teaspoon salt

2½ cups (10 ounces) confectioners' sugar

1 Using stand mixer fitted with paddle, beat butter, cream, vanilla, and salt on medium-high speed until smooth, about 1 minute. Reduce speed to medium-low, slowly add confectioners' sugar, and beat until incorporated and smooth, about 4 minutes.

2 Increase mixer speed to medium-high and beat until frosting is light and fluffy, about 5 minutes. (Frosting can be refrigerated for up to 3 days; let soften at room temperature, about 2 hours, then rewhip using mixer on medium speed until smooth, 2 to 5 minutes.)

# texas-style blueberry cobbler

serves 8 to 10

4 tablespoons unsalted butter, cut into 4 pieces, plus 8 tablespoons melted and cooled

1½ cups (10½ ounces) sugar

1½ teaspoons grated lemon zest

15 ounces (3 cups) blueberries

1½ cups (7½ ounces) all-purpose flour

2½ teaspoons baking powder

¾ teaspoon salt

1½ cups milk

1 Adjust oven rack to upper-middle position and heat oven to 350 degrees. Place 4 tablespoons cut-up butter in 13 by 9-inch baking dish and transfer to oven. Heat until butter is melted, 8 to 10 minutes.

2 Meanwhile, pulse ¼ cup sugar and lemon zest in food processor until combined, about 5 pulses; set aside. Using potato masher, mash blueberries and 1 tablespoon lemon sugar in bowl until berries are coarsely mashed.

3 Combine flour, baking powder, salt, and remaining 1¼ cups sugar in large bowl. Whisk in milk and 8 tablespoons melted, cooled butter until smooth. Remove baking dish from oven, transfer to wire rack, and pour batter into prepared pan.

4 Dollop mashed blueberry mixture evenly over batter, sprinkle with remaining lemon sugar, and bake until golden brown and edges are crisp, 45 to 50 minutes, rotating pan halfway through baking. Let cobbler cool on wire rack for 30 minutes. Serve warm.

# summer berry pie

serves 8

"

This recipe for Summer Berry Pie is an old ATK standard but I think it is one of the best pies we've ever made. It tastes like the best of summer, in a pie. There's no bouncy gelatin or dairy-heavy pudding to overshadow the fresh sweet-tart flavor of perfectly ripe berries. Rather, the filling is just fresh berries tossed with a handful of berries that have been cooked down with a little cornstarch to help hold things together. And the crust is just a cookie crust made with graham crackers, which I prefer to a traditional pie crust here because it has more flavor. Also, as with all of my favorite baked goods, the recipe is a breeze to make. The hardest part is buying ripe but firm berries that can withstand being washed without breaking apart. To wash the berries, I gently add them to a bowl of cold water and swish them around with my hands, then pull them out and let them dry in a single layer on a paper towel–lined baking sheet. This pie holds well for up to one day. Be sure to serve it with whipped cream. "

*julia*

## crust

8 whole graham crackers, broken into 1-inch pieces

3 tablespoons sugar

5 tablespoons unsalted butter, melted and cooled

## filling

10 ounces (2 cups) raspberries

10 ounces (2 cups) blackberries

10 ounces (2 cups) blueberries

½ cup (3½ ounces) sugar

3 tablespoons cornstarch

⅛ teaspoon salt

1 tablespoon lemon juice

2 tablespoons red currant or apple jelly

1  **For the crust**  Adjust oven rack to middle position and heat oven to 325 degrees. Process graham cracker pieces and sugar in food processor to fine, even crumbs, about 30 seconds. Sprinkle melted butter over crumbs and pulse to incorporate, about 5 pulses.

2  Sprinkle mixture into 9-inch pie plate. Using bottom of dry measuring cup, press crumbs into even layer on bottom and sides of pie plate. Bake until crust is fragrant and beginning to brown, 12 to 18 minutes; transfer to wire rack. Let cool completely.

3  **For the filling**  Gently toss berries together in large bowl. Process 2½ cups of berries in food processor until very smooth, about 1 minute (do not underprocess). Strain puree through fine-mesh strainer into small saucepan, pressing on solids to extract as much puree as possible (you should have about 1½ cups); discard solids.

4  Whisk sugar, cornstarch, and salt together in bowl, then whisk into strained puree. Bring puree mixture to boil, stirring constantly, and cook until it is as thick as pudding, about 7 minutes. Off heat, stir in lemon juice and let cool slightly.

5  Pour warm berry puree into cooled pie crust. Melt jelly in clean, dry small saucepan over low heat, then pour over remaining 3½ cups berries and toss to coat. Spread berries evenly over puree and lightly press them into puree. Cover pie loosely with plastic wrap and refrigerate until filling is chilled and set, at least 3 hours or up to 1 day. Serve chilled or at room temperature.

# apple galette

serves 10 to 12

### dough

1½ cups (7½ ounces) all-purpose flour

½ cup (2½ ounces) Wondra flour

½ teaspoon salt

½ teaspoon sugar

12 tablespoons unsalted butter, cut into ¼-inch pieces and chilled

7–9 tablespoons ice water

### topping

1½ pounds Granny Smith apples, peeled, cored, halved, and sliced ⅛ inch thick

2 tablespoons unsalted butter, cut into ¼-inch pieces

¼ cup (1¾ ounces) sugar

2 tablespoons apricot preserves

1 tablespoon water

1  **For the dough**  Process all-purpose flour, instant flour, salt, and sugar in food processor until combined, about 5 seconds. Scatter butter over top and pulse until mixture resembles coarse cornmeal, about 15 pulses. Continue to pulse, adding ice water 1 tablespoon at a time, until dough begins to form small curds that hold together when pinched with your fingers (dough will be crumbly), about 10 pulses.

2  Transfer dough crumbs to lightly floured counter and gather into rectangular-shaped pile. Starting at farthest end, use heel of your hand to smear small amount of dough against counter. Continue to smear dough until all crumbs have been worked. Gather smeared crumbs together in another rectangular-shaped pile and repeat process. Form dough into 4-inch square, wrap tightly in plastic wrap, and refrigerate for 1 hour. Let chilled dough sit on counter to soften slightly, about 10 minutes, before rolling. (Wrapped dough can be refrigerated for up to 2 days or frozen for up to 1 month. If frozen, let dough thaw completely on counter before rolling.)

3  Adjust oven rack to middle position and heat oven to 400 degrees. Cut piece of parchment paper to measure exactly 16 by 12 inches. Roll dough over parchment, dusting with flour as needed, until it just overhangs parchment. Trim edges of dough

even with parchment. Roll up outer 1 inch of dough to create ½-inch-thick border. Slide parchment with dough onto baking sheet.

**4 For the topping** Starting in 1 corner, shingle apple slices onto dough in tidy diagonal rows, overlapping them by one-third. Dot apple slices with butter and sprinkle evenly with sugar. Bake until bottom is deep golden brown and apples have caramelized, 45 minutes to 1 hour, rotating sheet halfway through baking. Transfer sheet to wire rack and let tart cool briefly.

**5** Microwave apricot preserves and water in bowl at 50 percent power until mixture begins to bubble, about 1 minute. Strain through fine-mesh strainer set over bowl, discarding large apricot pieces. Brush glaze evenly over apples and let cool for 10 minutes. Slide tart on parchment onto cutting board; discard parchment. Slice tart in half lengthwise, then crosswise into pieces. Serve warm or at room temperature.

# holiday celebrations

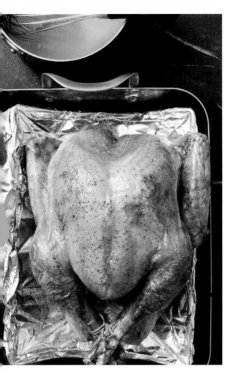

# smoked salmon with herbed crème fraîche

serves 8

4 ounces cream cheese

1 cup crème fraîche

3 tablespoons minced fresh dill

2 tablespoons minced fresh chives

2 teaspoons grated lemon zest plus 1 tablespoon juice

Salt and pepper

12 ounces thinly sliced smoked salmon, cut crosswise into 2- to 3-inch-long pieces

1 (9-ounce) bag kettle-cooked potato chips

Microwave cream cheese in bowl until very soft, 20 to 25 seconds. Whisk in crème fraîche, dill, chives, lemon zest and juice and season with salt and pepper to taste. Transfer to serving bowl, cover, and refrigerate for 20 minutes. Serve alongside salmon and potato chips. (Dip can be refrigerated in airtight container for up to 24 hours; season with additional lemon juice, salt, and pepper before serving.)

"
We always serve smoked salmon on special occasions and my default method for serving it (which I learned from my mother) is with sweet, whipped butter on pieces of dense German black bread. That is, until we developed this recipe for our menu cookbook a few years back (this book is still one of my all-time favorites). The lemony dip made with crème fraîche, dill, and chives is perfect with the salty potato chips, and the presentation is modern and casual. Cutting the salmon into smaller pieces is important so that they fit onto the potato chips. It's crucial to use kettle-cooked potato chips because they are sturdier than average and will support the weight of the toppings. "

*julia*

# classic shrimp cocktail

serves 8

"

Ian and I are known for our shrimp cocktail. In fact, it's not unusual for someone to ask us to bring it to their party (especially if they're family). The trick to the ultimate shrimp cocktail is twofold. First, buy good shrimp; domestic, untreated, shell-on shrimp is what we buy. Second, follow this simple recipe that builds a quick broth with water and Old Bay seasoning and then poaches the shrimp in it off the heat. This gentle cooking method ensures that the shrimp cook through evenly and are perfectly cooked and tender. Extra-large shrimp (21–25 count) work well here, but Ian prefers to use jumbo shrimp (16–20 count). For the sauce, buy refrigerated prepared horseradish, not the shelf-stable kind, which contains off-tasting preservatives and additives. "

*julia*

### shrimp

2 teaspoons lemon juice

2 bay leaves

1 teaspoon salt

1 teaspoon black peppercorns

1 teaspoon Old Bay seasoning

1 pound extra-large shrimp (21 to 25 per pound), peeled and deveined

### horseradish cocktail sauce

1 cup ketchup

2 tablespoons lemon juice

2 tablespoons prepared horseradish, plus extra for seasoning

2 teaspoons hot sauce, plus extra for seasoning

⅛ teaspoon salt

⅛ teaspoon pepper

1  **For the shrimp**  Bring lemon juice, bay leaves, salt, peppercorns, Old Bay, and 4 cups water to boil in medium saucepan for 2 minutes. Remove pan from heat and add shrimp. Cover and steep off heat until shrimp are firm and pink, about 7 minutes. Meanwhile, fill large bowl halfway with ice and water. Drain shrimp and plunge immediately into ice water to stop cooking; let sit until cool, about 2 minutes. Drain shrimp and transfer to bowl. Cover and refrigerate until thoroughly chilled, at least 1 hour.

2  **For the horseradish cocktail sauce**  Stir all ingredients together in small bowl and season with additional horseradish and hot sauce as desired. Arrange shrimp and sauce on serving platter or in individual dishes and serve. (Shrimp can be chilled for up to 24 hours after ice bath. Cocktail sauce can be refrigerated for up to 24 hours.)

# bacon and chive deviled eggs

makes 12 egg halves

2 slices bacon, chopped fine

1 recipe Easy-Peel Hard-Cooked Eggs (recipe follows)

2 tablespoons mayonnaise

1 teaspoon Dijon mustard

1 tablespoon minced fresh chives

2 teaspoons distilled white vinegar

⅛ teaspoon salt

Pinch cayenne pepper

**1** Cook bacon in 10-inch skillet over medium heat until crispy, 5 to 7 minutes. Using slotted spoon, transfer bacon to paper towel–lined plate. Reserve 1 tablespoon fat.

**2** Slice each egg in half length-wise with paring knife. Transfer yolks to bowl; arrange whites on serving platter. Mash yolks with fork until no large lumps remain. Add mayonnaise and mustard and use rubber spatula to smear mixture against side of bowl until thick, smooth paste forms, 1 to 2 minutes. Add reserved bacon fat, chives, vinegar, salt, and cayenne and mix until fully incorporated. Stir in three-quarters of bacon.

**3** Transfer yolk mixture to small heavy-duty plastic bag. Press mixture into 1 corner and twist top of bag. Using scissors, snip ½ inch off filled corner. Squeezing bag, distribute yolk mixture evenly among egg white halves. Sprinkle each egg half with remaining bacon and serve.

### easy-peel hard-cooked eggs

makes 6 eggs

6 large eggs

**1** Bring 1 inch water to rolling boil in medium saucepan over high heat. Place eggs in steamer basket. Transfer basket to saucepan. Cover, reduce heat to medium-low, and cook eggs for 13 minutes.

**2** When eggs are almost finished cooking, combine 2 cups ice cubes and 2 cups cold water in medium bowl. Using tongs or spoon, transfer eggs to ice bath; let sit for 15 minutes. Peel before using.

"

If you looked in my fridge right now, you'd find a batch of deviled eggs. Same thing last week, last month . . . you get the picture. Deviled eggs are one of my favorite snacks to have on hand, and they are also de rigueur on my Easter dinner table. What's great is that once you get the basic method of hard-cooking the eggs down pat (and this method really does produce easy-to-peel eggs), you can play around with fillings. Change up the herbs, or add chopped olives or pickles to the mix. Of course, my default filling contains bacon. Because . . . bacon. "

*bridget*

*Cooking at Home with Bridget and Julia*

228

# stuffed mushrooms with boursin and prosciutto

serves 8

" My wonderful childhood neighbors, the Paynes, first introduced me to easy stuffed mushrooms when I was 9 or 10, and I've loved them ever since. Their recipe, which I couldn't get enough of, involved putting a piece of cheddar and a dash of Worcestershire inside each mushroom cap and microwaving them until hot–hello, late 1970s! Fast-forward a few decades and I still love stuffed mushrooms but this recipe has long since replaced the Paynes' version as my all-time favorite. These mushrooms are parcooked in the microwave in order to help them exude some of their liquid before being stuffed and finished in the oven. The filling is simply some Boursin cheese (you can take the kid out of the '70s, but not the '70s out of the kid) along with some thinly sliced prosciutto and chives. Be sure to buy mushrooms with caps that measure between 1½ and 2 inches in diameter; they will shrink substantially as they roast. "

*julia*

24 (1½-to 2-inch-wide) white mushrooms, stems removed

2 tablespoons olive oil

Salt and pepper

1 (5.2-ounce) package Boursin Garlic & Fine Herbs cheese

2 thin slices (1 ounce) prosciutto, chopped

2 tablespoons chopped fresh parsley or chives

1 Adjust oven rack to lower-middle position and heat oven to 450 degrees. Toss mushrooms with oil and season with salt and pepper. Place mushrooms, gill side down, on plate lined with 2 layers of coffee filters. Microwave mushrooms until they release their moisture and shrink in size, about 10 minutes.

2 Line baking sheet with aluminum foil. Transfer mushrooms to prepared sheet, gill side up. Spoon Boursin into mushroom caps and sprinkle with prosciutto.

3 Bake mushrooms until cheese is hot and prosciutto begins to crisp, 10 to 12 minutes. Transfer to serving platter. Sprinkle with parsley or chives before serving.

# classic holiday cheddar cheese ball

serves 15 to 20

8 ounces extra-sharp cheddar cheese, shredded (2 cups)

8 ounces cream cheese, softened

2 tablespoons mayonnaise

1 tablespoon Worcestershire sauce

1 garlic clove, minced

¼ teaspoon cayenne pepper

½ cup sliced almonds, toasted

I don't know what it is about holiday entertaining, but for some reason I turn into a midcentury party hostess– a sort of Betty Draper without the cigarettes and psychosis–and serve retro food and cocktails in atomic-age dishware and glassware. Along with rumaki and fondue, you can bet that there's a cheese ball about. This version couldn't be easier to make, and it's so much better than the chalky, sour-tasting cheese balls that come already made. It's great to spread on homemade pita chips or crackers, but "Betty" and I know that good old salty Triscuits are the best cracker ever. ”

*bridget*

1  Process cheddar, cream cheese, mayonnaise, Worcestershire, garlic, and cayenne in food processor until smooth, about 1 minute, scraping down bowl as needed. Transfer mixture to center of large sheet of plastic wrap and twist plastic to shape cheese into rough ball; mixture will be somewhat loose. Refrigerate until firm, about 3 hours. (Cheese ball can be refrigerated for up to 2 days.)

2  Once cheese ball is firm, reshape as necessary until round and smooth. Unwrap, roll it in almonds, and let sit at room temperature for 15 minutes before serving.

## variations

### bacon-ranch cheese ball

Omit Worcestershire and cayenne. Add 3 tablespoons chopped fresh parsley, 3 tablespoons chopped fresh cilantro or fresh dill, 1 teaspoon lemon juice, ½ teaspoon onion powder, and pinch sugar to food processor in step 1. Substitute 6 slices bacon, cooked and crumbled, for almonds in step 2.

### antipasto cheese ball

Omit Worcestershire and cayenne. Substitute 1 cup shredded provolone and 1 cup shredded mozzarella for cheddar. Add 3 ounces thinly sliced deli salami, chopped; 2 tablespoons chopped jarred roasted red peppers; 2 tablespoons chopped jarred pepperoncini; and 2 tablespoons chopped fresh basil to food processor in step 1. Substitute ½ cup toasted pine nuts for almonds in step 2.

### beer cheese ball

Omit mayonnaise, Worcestershire, and cayenne. Add 3 tablespoons beer and 1 teaspoon yellow mustard to food processor in step 1. Substitute ½ cup crushed pretzels for almonds in step 2.

### lemon-herb goat cheese ball

Omit mayonnaise, Worcestershire, and cayenne. Substitute 2 cups crumbled goat cheese for cheddar. Add 2 tablespoons lemon juice, 2 tablespoons chopped fresh basil, and ½ teaspoon grated lemon zest to food processor in step 1. Substitute ½ cup finely chopped fresh chives for almonds in step 2.

# best prime rib and yorkshire puddings

serves 6 to 8

1 (7-pound) first-cut beef standing rib roast (3 bones)

Kosher salt and pepper

2 teaspoons vegetable oil

1  Using sharp knife, remove roast from bones, running knife down length of bones and following contours as closely as possible. Reserve bones. Cut slits spaced 1 inch apart in crosshatch pattern in fat cap, being careful to cut down to, but not into, meat. Rub 2 tablespoons salt all over roast and into slits. Place meat back on bones, transfer to large plate, and refrigerate, uncovered, for at least 24 hours or up to 4 days.

2  Adjust oven rack to middle position and heat oven to 200 degrees. Heat oil in 12-inch skillet over high heat until just smoking. Sear sides and top of roast (reserving bones) until browned, 6 to 8 minutes total (do not sear side where roast was cut from bones). Place meat back on ribs so bones fit where they were cut and let cool for 10 minutes. Tie roast to bones with 2 lengths of kitchen twine between ribs. Transfer roast, fat side up, to wire rack set in rimmed baking sheet and season with pepper. Roast until meat registers 110 degrees, 3 to 4 hours.

3  Turn off oven; leave roast in oven, opening door as little as possible, until meat registers about 120 degrees (for rare) or about 125 degrees (for medium-rare), 30 minutes to 1¼ hours longer.

4  Remove roast from oven (leave roast on sheet), tent with aluminum foil, and let rest for at least 30 minutes or up to 1¼ hours.

5  Adjust oven rack 8 inches from broiler element and heat broiler. Remove foil from roast, form into 3-inch ball, and place under ribs to elevate fat cap. Broil until top of roast is well browned and crispy, 2 to 8 minutes. Transfer roast to carving board. Remove twine and remove roast from ribs. Cut meat into ¾-inch-thick slices. Season with salt to taste, and serve.

## individual yorkshire puddings
makes 12

*Prepare the Yorkshire pudding batter after the beef has roasted for 2 hours, then, while the roast rests, add the beef fat to the batter and get the puddings into the oven.*

3 large eggs, room temperature

1½ cups whole milk, room temperature

1½ cups (7½ ounces) all-purpose flour

¾ teaspoon salt

3 tablespoons beef fat

**1** Whisk eggs and milk in large bowl until well combined, about 20 seconds. Whisk flour and salt in bowl and add to egg mixture; whisk quickly until flour is just incorporated and mixture is smooth, about 30 seconds. Cover batter with plastic wrap and let stand at room temperature for at least 1 hour or up to 3 hours.

**2** After removing roast from oven, whisk 1 tablespoon beef fat into batter until bubbly and smooth, about 30 seconds. Transfer batter to 1-quart liquid measuring cup or other pitcher.

**3** Measure ½ teaspoon beef fat into each cup of standard muffin pan. When roast is out of oven, increase temperature to 450 degrees and place pan in oven to heat for 3 minutes (fat will smoke). Working quickly, remove pan from oven, close oven door, and divide batter evenly among 12 muffin cups, filling each about two-thirds full. Immediately return pan to oven. Bake, without opening oven door, for 20 minutes; reduce oven temperature to 350 degrees and bake until deep golden brown, about 10 minutes longer. Remove pan from oven and pierce each pudding with skewer to release steam and prevent collapse. Using your hands or dinner knife, lift each pudding out of tin and serve immediately.

# roast beef tenderloin with persillade relish

serves 8

**"**

This hands-off tenderloin roast is my go-to recipe when I need an easy but elegant dinner that serves a crowd. The roast doesn't have to be served right away and still tastes great at room temperature if dinner gets delayed. The tricks are using a fairly hot oven (425 degrees), which gives the meat a little bit of a browned crust as it cooks through, and only cooking the meat to medium-rare. The parsley relish is the perfect sauce for this beef roast, or nearly any roast for that matter–it is one of my all-time favorite relishes and it can easily be made ahead of time. Consider using a food processor to mince the parsley. I almost always buy an untrimmed tenderloin because I like knife work, but there's no shame in ordering it pretrimmed to save time. Note that an untrimmed tenderloin will weigh 6 pounds or more. **"**

*julia*

*relish*

¾ cup minced fresh parsley

½ cup extra-virgin olive oil

6 tablespoons minced cornichons plus 1 teaspoon cornichon brine

¼ cup capers, rinsed and chopped coarse

2 scallions, minced

1 teaspoon sugar

Salt and pepper

*tenderloin*

1 (4½ - to 5-pound) whole beef tenderloin, trimmed, tail end tucked, and tied at 1½-inch intervals

2 tablespoons olive oil

Salt and pepper

**1** For the relish  Combine all ingredients in bowl and season with salt and pepper to taste. Let sit at room temperature until needed. (Relish can be refrigerated for up to 1 day; bring to room temperature before serving.)

**2** For the tenderloin  Adjust oven rack to upper-middle position and heat oven to 425 degrees. Set wire rack in aluminum foil–lined rimmed baking sheet. Pat tenderloin dry with paper towels, coat with oil, and season with salt and pepper. Lay tenderloin on prepared rack. (Prepped tenderloin can be held at room temperature for up to 1 hour before roasting.)

**3** Roast until tenderloin registers 120 to 125 degrees (for medium-rare), 45 minutes to 1 hour. Tent tenderloin with foil and let rest for 30 minutes. Transfer roast to carving board and remove twine. Slice meat into 1-inch-thick pieces and serve with relish.

# pressure-cooker pomegranate-braised boneless beef short ribs

serves 6

> Short ribs are a great option for company because they feel special and they can be made ahead of time. I like this recipe because it shortens the average 2-hour cooking time to just 35 minutes by using the pressure cooker, and replaces the expected red wine–based sauce with a modern, pomegranate-based one. Bacon adds a welcome smoky flavor and I like how this recipe strains it out before serving so that the sauce has a smooth, silky texture. Finishing the sauce with a hit of balsamic vinegar and a pat of butter really brings it to life. **"**

*julia*

2 slices bacon, chopped fine

1 onion, chopped fine

3 garlic cloves, minced

1½ cups unsweetened pomegranate juice

2 tablespoons packed brown sugar

4 (2-inch) strips orange zest plus ½ cup juice

2 sprigs fresh thyme

6 (8-ounce) boneless beef short ribs, trimmed

Salt and pepper

2 tablespoons balsamic vinegar

1½ tablespoons cornstarch

1 tablespoon unsalted butter

1  Cook bacon in pressure-cooker pot over medium-high heat until browned and crisp, about 3 minutes. Stir in onion and cook until softened, about 5 minutes. Stir in garlic and cook until fragrant, about 30 seconds. Stir in pomegranate juice, sugar, orange zest and juice, and thyme sprigs. Using wooden spoon, scrape up any browned bits stuck on bottom of pot. Pat short ribs dry with paper towels, season with salt and pepper, and nestle into pot.

2  Lock pressure-cooker lid in place and bring to high pressure over medium-high heat. As soon as pot reaches high pressure, reduce heat to medium-low and cook for 35 minutes, adjusting heat as needed to maintain high pressure.

3  Remove pot from heat and allow pressure to release naturally for 15 minutes. Quick-release any remaining pressure, then carefully remove lid, allowing steam to escape away from you.

4  Transfer short ribs to platter, tent with aluminum foil, and let rest while finishing sauce. Strain sauce into fat separator, let sit 5 minutes, then pour defatted sauce back into now-empty pot. Whisk vinegar and cornstarch together, then whisk into sauce and simmer over medium heat until thickened and measures 1½ cups, about 15 minutes. Off heat, whisk in butter and season with salt and pepper to taste. Serve sauce with ribs.

# home-corned beef and vegetables

serves 8 to 10

### corned beef

1 (4½- to 5-pound) beef brisket, flat cut

¾ cup salt

½ cup packed brown sugar

2 teaspoons pink curing kosher salt #1

6 garlic cloves, peeled

6 bay leaves

5 allspice berries

2 tablespoons black peppercorns

1 tablespoon coriander seeds

### vegetables

6 carrots, peeled, halved crosswise, thick ends halved lengthwise

1½ pounds small red potatoes, unpeeled

1 head green cabbage (2 pounds), uncored, cut into 8 wedges

1  **For the corned beef**  Trim fat on surface of brisket to ⅛ inch. Dissolve salt, sugar, and curing salt in 4 quarts water in large container. Add brisket, 3 garlic cloves, 4 bay leaves, allspice berries, 1 tablespoon peppercorns, and coriander seeds to brine. Weigh brisket down with plate, cover, and refrigerate for 6 days.

2  Adjust oven rack to middle position and heat oven to 275 degrees. Remove brisket from brine, rinse, and pat dry with paper towels. Cut 8-inch square triple thickness of cheesecloth. Place remaining

3 garlic cloves, remaining 2 bay leaves, and remaining 1 tablespoon peppercorns in center of cheesecloth and tie into bundle with kitchen twine. Place brisket, spice bundle, and 2 quarts water in Dutch oven. (Brisket may not lie flat but will shrink slightly as it cooks.)

3  Bring to simmer over high heat, cover, and transfer to oven. Cook until fork inserted into thickest part of brisket slides in and out with ease, 2½ to 3 hours.

4  Remove pot from oven and turn off oven. Transfer brisket to large ovensafe platter, ladle 1 cup of cooking liquid over meat, cover, and return to oven to keep warm.

5  **For the vegetables**  Add carrots and potatoes to pot and bring to simmer over high heat. Reduce heat to medium-low, cover, and simmer until vegetables begin to soften, 7 to 10 minutes.

6  Add cabbage to pot, increase heat to high, and return to simmer. Reduce heat to low, cover, and simmer until all vegetables are tender, 12 to 15 minutes.

7  While vegetables cook, transfer beef to cutting board and slice ¼ inch thick against grain. Return beef to platter. Using slotted spoon, transfer vegetables to platter with beef. Moisten with additional broth and serve.

# brown soda bread

makes 1 loaf

2 cups (10 ounces) all-purpose flour

1½ cups (8¼ ounces) whole-wheat flour

½ cup toasted wheat germ

3 tablespoons sugar

1½ teaspoons salt

1 teaspoon baking powder

1 teaspoon baking soda

1¾ cups buttermilk

3 tablespoons unsalted butter, melted

1 Adjust oven rack to lower-middle position and heat oven to 400 degrees. Line rimmed baking sheet with parchment paper.

2 Whisk all-purpose flour, whole-wheat flour, wheat germ, sugar, salt, baking powder, and baking soda together in large bowl. Combine buttermilk and 2 tablespoons melted butter in 2-cup liquid measuring cup. Add buttermilk mixture to flour mixture and stir with rubber spatula until dough just comes together.

3 Turn out dough onto lightly floured counter and knead until cohesive mass forms, about 8 times. Pat dough into 7-inch round and transfer to prepared sheet. Using sharp serrated knife, make ¼-inch-deep cross about 5 inches long on top of loaf.

4 Bake until skewer inserted in center comes out clean and loaf registers 195 degrees, 45 to 50 minutes, rotating sheet halfway through baking. Remove bread from oven. Brush with remaining 1 tablespoon melted butter. Transfer loaf to wire rack and let cool for at least 1 hour. Serve.

> Our offices at America's Test Kitchen are conveniently located near one of the Boston area's finest Irish pubs, so it's no rare occasion to spot some of my fellow coworkers enjoying themselves after work. The pub pulls one of the best pints of Guinness that you can find, and paired with a few hearty slices of soda bread, you can quickly fill your belly. This recipe for soda bread is my favorite. It's malty, wheaty, and has just the right whiff of baking soda to give it authentic flavor. Serve it with salted butter or a chunk of cheddar and pickles, and you've got yourself a meal.

*bridget*

# slow-roasted pork shoulder with peach sauce

serves 8 to 12

> I make this pork shoulder roast with peach sauce every December for our Davison family Christmas party. The roast has an incredible, tender texture and deep, porky flavor, but everyone's favorite part is the bronze, bacon-like fat cap on the top, which we all call 'candy.' The roast is rubbed with brown sugar and salt and then left to rest in the refrigerator overnight, which boosts browning and flavors the fat on top. As the roast rests on the counter after it's cooked, folks walk through the kitchen and pull off small pieces–thank goodness we're all family! Also, the fruity sauce with sweet and tart elements cuts the pork shoulder's richness. I often serve it with garlic mashed potatoes and braised red cabbage. The hardest part of this recipe is finding a bone-in pork butt; I usually have to call several stores to locate one. Pork butt roast is often labeled Boston butt in the supermarket. Add more water to the roasting pan as necessary to prevent the fond from burning.

*julia*

### pork roast

1 (6- to 8-pound) bone-in pork butt roast

⅓ cup kosher salt

⅓ cup packed light brown sugar

Pepper

### peach sauce

10 ounces frozen sliced peaches, cut into 1-inch chunks, or 2 fresh peaches, peeled, pitted, and cut into ½-inch wedges

2 cups dry white wine

½ cup granulated sugar

¼ cup plus 1 tablespoon rice vinegar

2 sprigs fresh thyme

1 tablespoon whole-grain mustard

1  **For the pork roast**  Using sharp knife, cut slits spaced 1 inch apart in crosshatch pattern in fat cap of roast, being careful to cut down to, but not into, meat. Combine salt and sugar in bowl. Rub salt mixture over entire pork shoulder and into slits. Wrap roast tightly in double layer of plastic wrap, place on rimmed baking sheet, and refrigerate for at least 12 or up to 24 hours.

2  Adjust oven rack to lowest position and heat oven to 325 degrees. Unwrap roast and brush any excess salt mixture from surface. Season roast with pepper. Spray V-rack with vegetable oil spray, set rack in large roasting pan, and place roast on rack. Add 1 quart water to roasting pan.

3  Roast pork, basting twice during cooking, until meat is extremely tender and meat near bone registers 190 degrees, 5 to 6 hours. Transfer roast to carving board, tent with aluminum foil, and let rest for 1 hour. Transfer liquid in roasting pan to fat separator and let sit for 5 minutes. Pour off ¼ cup jus and set aside for sauce; discard fat and remaining jus.

4  **For the peach sauce**  Simmer peaches, wine, sugar, ¼ cup vinegar, ¼ cup defatted jus, and thyme sprigs in small saucepan, stirring occasionally, until reduced to 2 cups, about 30 minutes. Off heat, discard thyme sprigs and stir in remaining 1 tablespoon vinegar and mustard; cover to keep warm.

5  Using sharp paring knife, cut around inverted T-shaped bone until it can be pulled free from roast (use clean dish towel to grasp bone). Using slicing knife, slice roast. Serve with sauce.

# cider baked ham

serves 16 to 20

1 cinnamon stick, broken into rough pieces

10 whole cloves

3¼ quarts apple cider

8 cups ice cubes

1 (7- to 10-pound) cured bone-in half ham, preferably shank end

2 tablespoons Dijon mustard

1 cup packed dark brown sugar

1 teaspoon pepper

Large oven bag

> I know that spiral-sliced hams are convenient to cook (just heat and serve; it's already sliced!), but I prefer to take the extra effort to find and purchase a cured ham that isn't presliced. One reason is that without all of those cuts made into the meat, more of the juices stay in the ham. The other, much more important reason is that you can buy an unsliced ham with the fat cap still attached. This recipe takes advantage of that by scoring the ham with a knife, roasting the meat, and then packing the exterior with a mix of brown sugar and black pepper. The result is a sticky, crispy, spicy-peppered crust of rendered pork crackling to fight over at the table. Oh, and there's really good ham inside! 99

*bridget*

1  Toast cinnamon and cloves in large saucepan over medium heat until fragrant, about 3 minutes. Add 4 cups cider and bring to boil. Pour spiced cider into large stockpot or clean bucket, add 4 cups cider and ice, and stir until melted.

2  Meanwhile, remove skin from exterior of ham and trim fat to ¼-inch thickness. Using sharp knife, cut slits spaced 1 inch apart in crosshatch pattern in surface layer of fat, being careful to cut down to, but not into, meat. Transfer ham to container with chilled cider mixture (liquid should nearly cover ham) and refrigerate for at least 4 hours or up to 12 hours.

3  Discard cider mixture and transfer ham to large oven bag. Add 1 cup fresh cider to bag, tie securely, and cut 4 slits in top of bag. Transfer to large roasting pan and let stand at room temperature for 1½ hours.

4  Adjust oven rack to lowest position and heat oven to 300 degrees. Bake until ham registers 100 degrees, 1½ to 2½ hours. Meanwhile, bring remaining 4 cups cider and mustard to boil in saucepan. Reduce heat to medium-low and simmer, stirring often, until mixture is very thick and reduced to ⅓ cup, about 1 hour.

5  Combine sugar and pepper in bowl. Remove ham from oven and let rest for 5 minutes. Increase oven temperature to 400 degrees. Roll back oven bag and brush ham with reduced cider mixture. Using your fingers, carefully press sugar mixture onto exterior of ham. Return to oven and bake until dark brown and caramelized, about 20 minutes. Transfer ham to carving board, tent with aluminum foil, and let rest for 15 minutes. Carve and serve.

# roast butterflied leg of lamb with coriander, cumin, and mustard seeds

serves 8 to 10

> I love serving lamb when we have company over because it feels more special than beef or pork. This recipe for leg of lamb is my favorite because the Mediterranean-style spiced oil and Lemon-Yogurt Sauce are a wonderful break from mint jelly (I hate mint jelly). The recipe is also incredibly fast for a large roast because the roast is butterflied—the total cooking/roasting time is less than 1 hour. I prefer to serve domestic, or American, lamb when serving a crowd because it has a milder flavor, although I personally love the stronger flavor of lamb imported from Australia.
>
> *julia*

1 (3½- to 4-pound) butterflied leg of lamb

Kosher salt

⅓ cup extra-virgin olive oil

3 shallots, sliced thin

4 garlic cloves, peeled and smashed

1 (1-inch) piece ginger, peeled, sliced into ½-inch-thick rounds, and smashed

1 tablespoon coriander seeds

1 tablespoon cumin seeds

1 tablespoon mustard seeds

3 bay leaves

2 (2-inch) strips lemon zest

1 recipe Lemon-Yogurt Sauce (recipe follows)

1  Place lamb on cutting board with fat cap facing down. Using sharp knife, trim any pockets of fat and connective tissue from underside of lamb. Flip lamb over, trim fat cap to between ⅛ and ¼ inch thick, and pound roast to even 1-inch thickness. Cut slits, spaced ½ inch apart, in fat cap in crosshatch pattern, being careful to cut down to, but not into, meat. Rub 1 tablespoon salt over entire roast and into slits. Let sit, uncovered, at room temperature for 1 hour.

2  Meanwhile, adjust oven rack to lower-middle position and second rack 4 to 5 inches from broiler element and heat oven to 250 degrees. Stir together oil, shallots, garlic, ginger, coriander seeds, cumin seeds, mustard seeds, bay leaves, and lemon zest in rimmed baking sheet and bake on lower rack until spices are softened and fragrant and shallots and garlic turn golden, about 1 hour. Remove sheet from oven and discard bay leaves.

3  Pat lamb dry with paper towels and transfer fat side up to sheet (directly on top of spices). Roast on lower rack until lamb registers 120 degrees, 20 to 25 minutes. Remove sheet from oven and heat broiler. Broil lamb on upper rack until surface is well browned and charred in spots and lamb registers 125 degrees (for medium-rare), 3 to 8 minutes.

4  Remove sheet from oven and transfer lamb to carving board (some spices will cling to bottom of roast). Tent with aluminum foil and let rest for 20 minutes.

5  Slice lamb with grain into 3 equal pieces. Turn each piece and slice against grain into ¼-inch-thick slices. Serve with sauce.

## lemon-yogurt sauce
makes about 1 cup

1 cup plain yogurt

1 tablespoon minced fresh mint

1 teaspoon grated lemon zest
plus 2 tablespoons juice

1 garlic clove, minced

Salt and pepper

Whisk yogurt, mint, lemon zest and juice, and garlic together in bowl until combined. Season with salt and pepper to taste. Let sit until flavors meld, about 30 minutes. (Sauce can be refrigerated for up to 2 days.)

*variations*
### roast butterflied leg of lamb with coriander, rosemary, and red pepper
Omit cumin and mustard seeds. Toss 6 sprigs fresh rosemary and ½ teaspoon red pepper flakes with oil mixture in step 2.

### roast butterflied leg of lamb with coriander, fennel, and black pepper
Substitute 1 tablespoon fennel seeds for cumin seeds and 1 tablespoon black peppercorns for mustard seeds.

# oven-roasted salmon fillets with almond vinaigrette

serves 8

"

When in doubt, serve salmon! That's my motto when I've got new friends coming for dinner, I'm serving a large crowd, or I'm heading to a potluck. This recipe, which roasts the fish in just 10 minutes, is the best. Also, I've found that this salmon tastes great cold so it's perfect for a brunch or buffet. The almond vinaigrette is a somewhat surprising flavor that pairs well with the fish and is very elegant. When making the vinaigrette, be aware that its consistency should be thick and clingy. Sometimes I cut the fillets in half widthwise into smaller portions for large crowds or buffets; obviously, these smaller pieces cook more quickly. It is important to keep the salmon skin on during cooking; however, you can remove it before serving if you want. "

*julia*

### almond vinaigrette

½ cup whole almonds, toasted

1 shallot, minced

3 tablespoons white wine vinegar

4 teaspoons honey

2 teaspoons Dijon mustard

⅔ cup extra-virgin olive oil

3 tablespoons water, plus extra as needed

2 tablespoons minced fresh tarragon

Salt and pepper

### salmon

2 (2-pound) skin-on salmon fillets, about 1½ inches thick

4 teaspoons olive oil

Salt and pepper

**1** For the almond vinaigrette Place almonds in zipper-lock bag and pound with rolling pin until coarsely crushed. Whisk crushed almonds, shallot, vinegar, honey, and mustard in medium bowl. Whisking constantly, drizzle in olive oil. Whisk in water and tarragon and season with salt and pepper to taste.

**2** For the salmon  Use sharp knife to remove any whitish fat from belly of salmon and cut each fillet into 4 equal pieces. Using sharp (or serrated) knife, cut 4 shallow slashes, about 1 inch apart, through skin of each fillet (do not cut into flesh). Pat salmon dry with paper towels and rub with oil. (Prepped salmon can be refrigerated for up to 24 hours before cooking.)

**3** Adjust oven rack to lowest position, place rimmed baking sheet on rack, and heat oven to 500 degrees. Season salmon with salt and pepper. Reduce oven temperature to 275 degrees and remove hot baking sheet. Carefully lay salmon, skin side down, on hot sheet. Roast until center is still translucent when checked with tip of paring knife and registers 125 degrees (for medium-rare), 9 to 13 minutes.

**4** Transfer fillets to individual plates or platter, spoon vinaigrette over top, and serve.

# classic roast turkey

serves 10 to 22

Salt and pepper

1 (12- to 22-pound) turkey, fully thawed if frozen, neck and giblets removed and reserved for gravy (optional)

2 onions, chopped coarse

2 carrots, peeled and chopped coarse

2 celery ribs, chopped coarse

2 tablespoons minced fresh thyme or 2 teaspoons dried

4 tablespoons unsalted butter, melted

1 cup chicken broth, as needed

1  For a 12- to 17-pound turkey, dissolve 1 cup salt in 2 gallons water in large container or bowl. Submerge turkey completely in brine. Cover and refrigerate for 6 to 12 hours. (If your turkey weighs 18 to 22 pounds, increase salt to 1 ½ cups and increase water to 3 gallons. Brining time is the same.) Remove turkey from brine and pat dry with paper towels.

2  Adjust oven rack to lowest position and heat oven to 425 degrees. Trim tailpiece, tie legs together, and tuck wings under bird. Chop neck and giblets into 1-inch pieces if using them for gravy.

3  Spread onions, carrots, celery, and thyme in large roasting pan. Line V-rack with heavy-duty aluminum foil and poke several holes in foil. Set rack inside roasting pan and spray foil with vegetable oil spray.

4  Brush breast side of turkey with half of butter and season with salt and pepper. Lay turkey in rack breast side down. Brush back of turkey with remaining butter and season with salt and pepper. Roast turkey for 1 hour.

5  Remove turkey from oven. Lower oven temperature to 325 degrees. Tip juice from cavity of turkey into pan. Flip turkey breast side up using clean dish towels or wads of paper towels. Continue to roast turkey until thickest portion of breast registers 160 degrees and thigh registers 175 degrees, 1 to 2 ½ hours longer. (Add broth as needed to prevent drippings from burning.)

6  Tip turkey so that juice from cavity runs into roasting pan. Transfer turkey to carving board and let rest, uncovered, for 30 minutes. (Meanwhile, use roasted vegetables and drippings in pan to make gravy, if desired.) Carve and serve.

> My little family has two Thanksgiving meals; the first official Thanksgiving meal with lots of family and a nicely set table, and a second, unofficial meal at my house just for Ian, Marta, and me. We celebrate twice because Ian and Marta both love turkey with gravy, and we like to have lots of leftovers on hand for 'gobbler' sandwiches. There are many great turkey recipes out there, but I like this one because it's simple, stress-free, and bombproof. I usually buy a kosher bird so I can avoid the step of brining or salting, and I don't feel obligated to flip the bird over during roasting if it's too big or I'm not in the mood (in which case, I just start it breast side up). Depending on the size of the turkey, your total roasting time will vary from 2 to 3½ hours.

*julia*

# slow-roasted turkey with gravy

serves 10 to 12

Do you have a family that only eats turkey breast? Or maybe there aren't enough turkey drumsticks to go around on Thanksgiving Day. That's why I love this recipe—you get to 'build' the turkey yourself with turkey parts. In fact, you don't even need to brine or salt the meat before cooking. The key is slow-roasting the parts so that the juices stay inside the meat. For all of the folks that have ever asked me how to make Thanksgiving dinner less stressful, this one is for you. "

*bridget*

## turkey

3 onions, chopped

3 celery ribs, chopped

2 carrots, peeled and chopped

5 sprigs fresh thyme

5 garlic cloves, peeled and halved

1 cup chicken broth

1 (5-to 7-pound) bone-in whole turkey breast, trimmed

4 pounds turkey drumsticks and thighs, trimmed

3 tablespoons unsalted butter, melted

1 tablespoon salt

2 teaspoons pepper

## gravy

2 cups chicken broth

3 tablespoons unsalted butter

3 tablespoons all-purpose flour

2 bay leaves

Salt and pepper

**1  For the turkey**  Adjust oven rack to lower-middle position and heat oven to 275 degrees. Arrange onions, celery, carrots, thyme sprigs, and garlic in even layer in rimmed baking sheet. Pour broth into sheet. Place wire rack on top of vegetables.

**2**  Pat turkey pieces dry with paper towels. Brush turkey pieces on all sides with melted butter and sprinkle with salt and pepper. Place breast skin side down and drumsticks and thighs skin side up on wire rack in vegetable-filled sheet, leaving at least ¼ inch between turkey pieces.

**3**  Roast turkey pieces for 1 hour. Using 2 large wads of paper towels, turn turkey breast skin side up. Continue to roast until breast registers 160 degrees and drumsticks/thighs register 175 degrees, 1 to 2 hours longer. Remove sheet from oven and transfer wire rack with turkey to second rimmed baking sheet. Let turkey rest for at least 30 minutes or up to 1 ½ hours.

**4  For the gravy**  Strain vegetables and liquid from sheet through fine-mesh strainer set in 4-cup liquid measuring cup, pressing on solids to extract as much liquid as possible; discard solids. Add broth to measuring cup (you should have about 3 cups liquid).

**5**  Melt butter in medium saucepan over medium-high heat. Add flour and cook, stirring constantly, until flour is dark golden brown and fragrant, about 5 minutes. Slowly whisk in broth mixture and bay leaves and gradually bring to boil. Reduce heat to simmer and cook, stirring occasionally, until gravy is thick and measures 2 cups, 15 to 20 minutes. Discard bay leaves. Off heat, season gravy with salt and pepper to taste. Cover to keep warm.

**6**  Heat oven to 500 degrees. Place sheet with turkey in oven. Roast until skin is golden brown and crispy, about 15 minutes. Transfer turkey to carving board and let rest, uncovered, for 20 minutes. Carve and serve with gravy.

*Holiday Celebrations*

# cornbread and sausage stuffing

serves 10 to 12

12 cups cornbread, broken into 1-inch pieces (include crumbs)

3 cups chicken broth

2 cups half-and-half

2 large eggs, lightly beaten

8 tablespoons unsalted butter, plus extra for baking dish

1½ pounds bulk pork sausage, broken into 1-inch pieces

3 onions, chopped fine

3 celery ribs, chopped fine

2 tablespoons minced fresh thyme

2 tablespoons minced fresh sage

3 garlic cloves, minced

1 tablespoon kosher salt

2 teaspoons pepper

1  Adjust oven racks to upper-middle and lower-middle positions and heat oven to 250 degrees. Spread cornbread evenly over 2 rimmed baking sheets. Bake until dry, 50 minutes to 1 hour, switching and rotating sheets halfway through baking. Transfer cornbread to large bowl.

2  Whisk together broth, half-and-half, and eggs in medium bowl; pour over cornbread and toss very gently to coat. Set aside.

3  Melt 2 tablespoons butter in 12-inch skillet over medium-high heat; swirl to coat pan bottom. Add sausage and cook, stirring occasionally, until sausage loses its raw color, 5 to 7 minutes. With slotted spoon, transfer sausage to medium bowl. Add half of onions and celery to fat in skillet and cook, stirring occasionally, over medium-high heat until softened, about 5 minutes. Transfer onion mixture to bowl with sausage. Melt remaining 6 tablespoons butter in now-empty skillet over medium-high heat. Add remaining celery and onions and cook, stirring occasionally, until softened, about 5 minutes. Stir in thyme, sage, and garlic and cook until fragrant, about 30 seconds; add salt and pepper. Add onion-celery mixture and sausage-onion mixture to cornbread and stir gently to combine. Cover bowl with plastic wrap and refrigerate to blend flavors, at least 1 hour or up to 4 hours.

4  Adjust oven rack to lower-middle position and heat oven to 400 degrees. Butter 15 by 10-inch baking dish (or two 9-inch square or 11 by 7-inch baking dishes). Transfer stuffing to baking dish; pour any liquid accumulated in bottom of bowl over stuffing and, if necessary, gently press stuffing with rubber spatula to fit into baking dish. Bake on lower rack until golden brown, 35 to 40 minutes. Serve.

> When I moved to the Northeast, it took awhile to understand the local lingo. A drinking fountain is called a 'bubbler' and 'wicked' is a positive thing. But no matter how long I live here, the side dish made of bread that you serve with the Thanksgiving turkey is called 'dressing' not 'stuffing.' (It's only stuffing if you stuff it IN the turkey!) And it should be made of cornbread, not sandwich bread. Sadly for me, I lost the dressing/stuffing battle when we named this recipe, but no matter what it's called, this cornbread and sausage dish has been on my Thanksgiving table for the last 17 years.

*bridget*

# potato and fennel gratin

serves 8

2½ pounds russet potatoes, peeled and sliced ⅛ inch thick

1 large fennel bulb, 1 tablespoon fronds minced, stalks discarded, bulb halved, cored, and sliced thin

2 tablespoons unsalted butter

2 shallots, minced

1½ teaspoons salt

3 garlic cloves, minced

2 teaspoons minced fresh thyme

¼ teaspoon fennel seeds, crushed

¼ teaspoon pepper

⅛ teaspoon ground nutmeg

⅛ teaspoon cayenne pepper

1 tablespoon all-purpose flour

1½ cups heavy cream

3 ounces Gruyère or Parmesan cheese, grated (1½ cups)

> The addition of fresh fennel, fennel seeds, and thyme to this traditional potato gratin adds wonderful sweet flavor and a little sophistication. Also, it has foolproof make-ahead instructions, which are super-valuable when planning a nice dinner for company. Slicing the potatoes ⅛ inch thick is crucial for the success of this dish; use a mandoline, a V-slicer, or a food processor fitted with a ⅛-inch-thick slicing blade. But don't be tempted to store the sliced potatoes in water to prevent browning or the gratin will turn out watery.
>
> *julia*

1 Adjust oven rack to middle position and heat oven to 350 degrees. Thoroughly grease shallow 2- or 3-quart casserole dish. Place potatoes and fennel in very large bowl.

2 Melt butter in small saucepan over medium heat. Add shallots and salt and cook until softened, about 2 minutes. Stir in garlic, thyme, fennel seeds, pepper, nutmeg, and cayenne and cook until fragrant, about 30 seconds. Stir in flour and cook for 1 minute. Whisk in cream, bring to simmer, and cook until thickened, about 2 minutes.

3 Pour sauce over potatoes and fennel and toss to coat. Transfer mixture to prepared dish and gently pack into even layer, removing any air pockets. Cover dish with aluminum foil and bake until potatoes are tender (paring knife can be slipped in and out of potato slice with some resistance), about 1¾ hours, rotating dish halfway through baking.

4 Transfer gratin to wire rack and remove foil. (Gratin can be wrapped tightly and refrigerated for up to 2 days; let sit at room temperature for 1 hour before continuing.)

5 Increase oven temperature to 450 degrees. Sprinkle Gruyère evenly over top of casserole. Bake until cheese is golden brown and sauce is bubbling around edges, 15 to 20 minutes. Let cool for 10 minutes, sprinkle with fennel fronds, and serve.

# holiday scalloped potatoes

serves 8 to 10

2 tablespoons unsalted butter

1 small onion, chopped fine

2 garlic cloves, minced

3 cups heavy cream

1 cup whole milk

4 sprigs fresh thyme

2 bay leaves

2 teaspoons salt

½ teaspoon pepper

4 pounds russet potatoes, peeled and cut into ⅛-inch-thick slices

4 ounces cheddar cheese, shredded (1 cup)

> I love that these are called 'Holiday Scalloped Potatoes,' as if I only make and serve them for the holidays–ha! These tender, saucy potatoes are as perfect served next to weeknight pork chops as they are alongside a big ham or leg of lamb. Since the potatoes are parboiled in milk and cream, the total cooking time is just over 30 minutes. For our family of four, I often cut the recipe in half and bake the potatoes in a 9-inch square baking dish.

*bridget*

1  Adjust oven rack to middle position and heat oven to 350 degrees. Melt butter in Dutch oven over medium-high heat. Add onion and cook until softened and beginning to brown, about 4 minutes. Add garlic and cook until fragrant, about 30 seconds. Add cream, milk, thyme sprigs, bay leaves, salt, pepper, and potatoes and bring to simmer. Cover, adjusting heat as necessary to maintain light simmer, and cook until potatoes are almost tender (paring knife can be slipped in and out of potato slice with some resistance), about 15 minutes.

2  Discard thyme sprigs and bay leaves. Transfer potato mixture to 3-quart gratin dish and sprinkle with cheddar. Bake until bubbling around edges and top is golden brown, about 20 minutes. Let cool for 5 minutes before serving.

# roasted winter squash with tahini and feta

serves 6

3 pounds butternut squash

3 tablespoons extra-virgin olive oil

Salt and pepper

1 tablespoon tahini

1½ teaspoons lemon juice

1 teaspoon honey

1 ounce feta cheese, crumbled
(¼ cup)

¼ cup shelled pistachios, toasted
and chopped fine

2 tablespoons chopped
fresh mint

"

I make roasted winter squash all the time, but I love to make this dressed-up version with tahini, pistachios, and feta for company because it's unexpected and a real looker. Also, this dish tastes great warm or at room temperature, which makes it easy to serve. The hardest part of this recipe is cutting up the butternut squash, but how it's cut makes all the difference in terms of how the squash cooks and how it looks on the platter. For the best texture, be sure to peel the squash thoroughly, removing all of the fibrous flesh just below the skin. "

*julia*

1  Adjust oven rack to lowest position and heat oven to 425 degrees. Using sharp vegetable peeler or chef's knife, remove squash skin and fibrous threads just below skin (squash should be completely orange with no white flesh). Halve squash lengthwise and scrape out seeds. Place squash cut side down on cutting board and slice crosswise into ½-inch-thick pieces.

2  Toss squash with 2 tablespoons oil, ½ teaspoon salt, and ½ teaspoon pepper and arrange in rimmed baking sheet in single layer. Roast squash until sides touching sheet toward back of oven are well browned, 25 to 30 minutes. Rotate sheet and continue to roast until sides touching sheet toward back of oven are well browned, 6 to 10 minutes.

3  Use metal spatula to flip each piece and continue to roast until squash is very tender and sides touching sheet are browned, 10 to 15 minutes.

4  Transfer squash to serving platter. Whisk tahini, lemon juice, honey, remaining 1 tablespoon oil, and pinch salt together in bowl. Drizzle squash with tahini dressing and sprinkle with feta, pistachios, and mint. Serve.

# arugula salad with prosciutto, figs, and parmesan

serves 6

¼ cup extra-virgin olive oil

2 ounces thinly sliced prosciutto, cut into ¼-inch-wide ribbons

3 tablespoons balsamic vinegar

1 tablespoon raspberry jam

1 small shallot, minced

Salt and pepper

½ cup dried figs, stemmed and chopped

8 ounces (8 cups) baby arugula

½ cup walnuts, toasted and chopped

2 ounces Parmesan cheese, shaved

1  Heat 1 tablespoon oil in 10-inch nonstick skillet over medium heat. Add prosciutto and cook, stirring often, until crisp, about 7 minutes. Using slotted spoon, transfer prosciutto to paper towel–lined plate; set aside.

2  Whisk vinegar, jam, shallot, ¼ teaspoon salt, and ⅛ teaspoon pepper together in large bowl. Stir in figs, cover, and microwave until steaming, about 1 minute. Whisking constantly, slowly drizzle in remaining 3 tablespoons oil. Let sit until figs are softened and vinaigrette has cooled to room temperature, about 15 minutes.

3  Just before serving, whisk vinaigrette to re-emulsify. Add arugula and gently toss to coat. Season with salt and pepper to taste. Serve, topping individual portions with prosciutto, walnuts, and Parmesan.

> Some folks might be surprised that I eat a lot of vegetables. Yes, it's true—every meal I serve features at least one vegetable side, and this salad is often one of those sides. I love that each bite is an explosion of textures and flavors. Peppery baby arugula is tossed with crisp prosciutto and crunchy walnuts, chewy figs softened in a homemade raspberry dressing, and shingles of salty Parmesan. It's a salad dressed to impress.

*bridget*

# brussels sprout salad
# with pecorino and pine nuts

serves 8

3 tablespoons lemon juice

2 tablespoons Dijon mustard

1 small shallot, minced

1 garlic clove, minced

Salt and pepper

6 tablespoons extra-virgin olive oil

2 pounds Brussels sprouts, trimmed, halved, and sliced very thin

3 ounces Pecorino Romano cheese, shredded (1 cup)

½ cup pine nuts, toasted

1 Whisk lemon juice, mustard, shallot, garlic, and ½ teaspoon salt together in large bowl. Whisking constantly, drizzle in oil. Add Brussels sprouts, toss to combine, and let sit for at least 30 minutes or up to 2 hours.

2 Stir in Pecorino and pine nuts. Season with salt and pepper to taste, and serve.

> This salad is a labor of love. It takes some serious time to slice up all the Brussels sprouts (even for me, and I'm fast with a knife) but it's worth it. The food processor can do it for you in a pinch, but it slices them very unevenly. Besides setting time aside for knife work, the key to this salad is letting the Brussels sprouts marinate and soften in a bright vinaigrette made with lemon juice and Dijon mustard for 30 minutes. The addition of toasted pine nuts and shredded Pecorino Romano makes this simple salad feel luxurious. Be sure to shred the Pecorino Romano on a coarse grater.

*julia*

# roasted brussels sprouts with bacon and pecans

serves 6 to 8

2¼ pounds Brussels sprouts, trimmed and halved

5 tablespoons olive oil

1 tablespoon water

Salt and pepper

4 slices bacon

½ cup finely chopped pecans, toasted

1 Adjust oven rack to upper-middle position and heat oven to 500 degrees. Toss Brussels sprouts, 3 tablespoons oil, water, ¾ teaspoon salt, and ¼ teaspoon pepper in large bowl until sprouts are coated. Transfer Brussels sprouts to rimmed baking sheet and arrange so cut sides are facing down. Cover sheet tightly with aluminum foil and roast for 10 minutes.

2 Cook bacon in 10-inch skillet over medium heat until crisp, 7 to 10 minutes. Transfer bacon to paper towel–lined plate and reserve 1 tablespoon bacon fat. Chop bacon fine.

3 Remove foil and continue to cook Brussels sprouts until they are well browned and tender, 10 to 12 minutes. Transfer to serving platter and toss with remaining 2 tablespoons oil, reserved bacon fat, chopped bacon, and pecans. Season with salt and pepper to taste, and serve.

# broiled asparagus
# with lemon-shallot vinaigrette

serves 6 to 8

2 pounds thin asparagus, trimmed

⅓ cup plus 1 tablespoon extra-virgin olive oil

Salt and pepper

1 large shallot, minced

1 teaspoon grated lemon zest plus 1 tablespoon juice

1 tablespoon minced fresh thyme

¼ teaspoon Dijon mustard

**1** Adjust oven rack 4 inches from broiler element and heat broiler.

**2** Toss asparagus with 1 tablespoon oil and season with salt and pepper, then lay spears in single layer on rimmed baking sheet. Broil until asparagus is tender and lightly browned, 8 to 10 minutes, shaking sheet halfway through broiling to turn spears.

**3** Let asparagus cool for 5 minutes and arrange on serving dish.

**4** Whisk shallot, lemon zest and juice, thyme, mustard, and remaining ⅓ cup oil in small bowl; season with salt and pepper to taste. Drizzle over asparagus and serve immediately.

> People ask me how they can get their kids to eat (or try) vegetables. Believe me, I can relate. My two boys are pretty good vegetable eaters now, but it wasn't always so. I tried a whole bunch of cooking methods—boiling, sautéing, and steaming. I also tried various method of culinary deception—blanketing the veg under tidal waves of cheese sauce, or chopping the veg into such infinitesimal pieces that they could never be detected in a tomato sauce (spoiler alert—kids can and will find vegetables in anything). But like the moment that you realize your best friend is the love of your life, I too found eternal happiness in the form of my oven broiler. Like a magic box that transforms raw, gross, disgusting vegetables (my kids' words, not mine) into charred, tender, slightly sweet side dishes, the broiler was my newfound kitchen love, and it was right there all along.

*bridget*

# rustic walnut tart

serves 8

"

People often ask me if I'm more of a baker or a cook–I'm definitely more of a cook. Not that I can't bake, but rather I get impatient when I have to fuss over things to make them look pretty, like decorating a cake. Tarts, however, are right up my alley because they can be made ahead of time and they always look attractive. This simple, elegant walnut tart is a favorite of mine because the balance of walnuts, vanilla, and bourbon is pure perfection. (Also, Ian is some-what of a bourbon aficionado so we always have a few good bottles on hand.) This tart crust is my go-to because it doesn't have to be rolled out; you simply press it into the tart pan and go. Don't skip the bourbon whipped cream–it's the perfect finishing touch. "

*julia*

### crust

1 cup (5 ounces) all-purpose flour

⅓ cup packed (2⅓ ounces) light brown sugar

¼ cup walnuts, toasted and chopped coarse

1 teaspoon salt

¼ teaspoon baking powder

6 tablespoons unsalted butter, cut into ½-inch pieces and chilled

### filling

½ cup packed (3½ ounces) light brown sugar

⅓ cup light corn syrup

4 tablespoons unsalted butter, melted and cooled

1 tablespoon bourbon or dark rum

2 teaspoons vanilla extract

½ teaspoon salt

1 large egg

1¾ cups walnuts, chopped coarse

### whipped cream

1 cup heavy cream, chilled

¼ cup bourbon or dark rum (optional)

1 tablespoon granulated sugar

¼ teaspoon vanilla extract

Pinch salt

1  **For the crust**  Grease 9-inch tart pan with removable bottom. Pulse flour, sugar, walnuts, salt, and baking powder in food processor until combined, about 5 pulses. Sprinkle butter over top and pulse until mixture is pale yellow and resembles coarse cornmeal, about 8 pulses.

2  Sprinkle mixture into prepared pan. Press crumbs firmly into even layer over pan bottom and up sides using bottom of dry measuring cup. Set tart pan on large plate, cover with plastic wrap, and freeze for at least 30 minutes or up to 1 week.

3  Adjust oven rack to middle position and heat oven to 350 degrees. Set tart pan on baking sheet. Press double layer aluminum foil into frozen tart shell and over edges of pan and fill with pie weights. Bake until tart shell is golden brown and set, about 30 minutes, rotating sheet halfway through baking. Let tart shell cool slightly while making filling.

4  **For the filling**  Whisk sugar, corn syrup, melted butter, bourbon, vanilla, and salt in large bowl until sugar dissolves. Whisk in egg until combined. Pour filling evenly into tart shell and sprinkle with walnuts. Bake until filling is set and walnuts begin to brown, 30 to 40 minutes, rotating sheet halfway through baking. Let tart cool completely, about 2 hours. (Tart can be refrigerated for up to 2 days; bring to room temperature before serving.)

**5 For the whipped cream** Using stand mixer fitted with whisk, whip cream, bourbon, if using, sugar, vanilla, and salt on medium-low speed until foamy, about 1 minute. Increase speed to high and whip until soft peaks form, 1 to 3 minutes. (Whipped cream can be refrigerated for up to 8 hours; rewhisk briefly before serving.)

**6** To serve, remove outer ring from tart pan, slide thin metal spatula between tart and tart pan bottom, and carefully slide tart onto serving platter or cutting board. Slice tart into wedges and serve with whipped cream.

# pecan pie

serves 8

### dough

1¼ cups (6¼ ounces) all-purpose flour

1 tablespoon granulated sugar

½ teaspoon salt

6 tablespoons unsalted butter, cut into ¼-inch pieces and chilled

4 tablespoons vegetable shortening, cut into 2 pieces and chilled

2 tablespoons vodka, chilled

2 tablespoons ice water

### filling

6 tablespoons unsalted butter, cut into 1-inch pieces

1 cup packed (7 ounces) dark brown sugar

½ teaspoon salt

3 large eggs

¾ cup light corn syrup

1 tablespoon vanilla extract

2 cups pecans, toasted and chopped fine

**1 For the dough** Process ¾ cup flour, sugar, and salt in food processor until combined, about 5 seconds. Scatter butter and shortening over top and continue to process until incorporated and mixture begins to form uneven clumps with no remaining floury bits, about 10 seconds.

**2** Scrape down sides of bowl and redistribute dough evenly around processor blade. Sprinkle remaining ½ cup flour over dough and pulse until mixture has broken up into pieces and is evenly distributed around bowl, 4 to 6 pulses.

**3** Transfer mixture to medium bowl. Sprinkle vodka and ice water over mixture. Using stiff rubber spatula, stir and press dough until it sticks together.

**4** Turn dough onto sheet of plastic wrap and form into 4-inch disk. Wrap tightly in plastic and refrigerate for at least 1 hour. Let chilled dough sit on counter to soften slightly, about 10 minutes, before rolling. (Wrapped dough can be refrigerated for up to 2 days or frozen for up to 1 month. If frozen, let dough thaw completely on counter before rolling.)

**5** Adjust oven rack to lowest position and heat oven to 425 degrees. Roll dough into 12-inch circle on floured counter. Loosely roll dough around rolling pin and gently unroll it onto 9-inch pie plate, letting excess dough hang over edge. Ease dough into plate by gently lifting edge of dough with your hand while pressing into plate bottom with your other hand. Wrap dough-lined plate loosely in plastic and refrigerate until dough is firm, about 30 minutes.

**6** Trim overhang to ½ inch beyond lip of plate. Tuck overhang under itself; folded edge should be flush with edge of plate. Crimp dough evenly around edge of plate using your fingers. Wrap dough-lined plate loosely in plastic and refrigerate until dough is firm, about 15 minutes, before using.

**7** Line chilled pie shell with parchment paper or double layer of aluminum foil, covering edges to prevent burning, and fill with pie weights.

**8** Bake until pie dough looks dry and is pale in color, about 15 minutes. Remove parchment and weights and continue to bake crust until light golden brown, 4 to 7 minutes longer. Transfer plate to wire rack. (Crust must still be warm when filling is added.)

**9** **For the filling** While crust is baking, melt butter in heatproof bowl set over saucepan filled with 1 inch barely simmering water, making sure that water does not touch bottom of bowl. Off heat, stir in sugar and salt until butter is absorbed. Whisk in eggs, then corn syrup and vanilla, until smooth. Return bowl to saucepan and stir until mixture is shiny, hot to touch, and registers 130 degrees. Off heat, stir in pecans.

**10** As soon as pie crust comes out of oven, adjust oven rack to lower-middle position and reduce oven temperature to 275 degrees. Pour pecan mixture into warm crust. Place pie on rimmed baking sheet and bake until filling looks set but yields like gelatin when gently pressed with back of spoon, 50 minutes to 1 hour, rotating sheet halfway through baking. Let pie cool on wire rack until filling has set, about 2 hours; serve slightly warm or at room temperature. (Cooled pie can be wrapped tightly in foil and stored at room temperature for up to 2 days.)

# chocolate pots de crème

serves 8

### pots de crème

10 ounces bittersweet chocolate, chopped fine

1 tablespoon vanilla extract

1 tablespoon water

½ teaspoon instant espresso powder

5 large egg yolks

5 tablespoons (2¼ ounces) sugar

¼ teaspoon salt

1½ cups heavy cream

¾ cup half-and-half

### whipped cream and garnish

½ cup heavy cream, chilled

2 teaspoons sugar

½ teaspoon vanilla extract

Cocoa powder and/or chocolate shavings (optional)

"

This is, hands down, the ultimate dessert for a party because it's easy, it can be made ahead, and it tastes incredible. Using the right chocolate, however, is crucial; I always use Ghirardelli bittersweet chocolate with 60 percent cacao (a winning brand in the test kitchen) because it helps the custard set up perfectly smooth. For large parties, I ditch the ramekins and portion the custard into tiny plastic shot glasses (from the party store, along with tiny silver plastic spoons for serving). For special occasions, I top the custards with a thin layer of dulce de leche before refrigerating. "

*julia*

1 **For the pots de crème** Place chocolate in medium bowl and set fine-mesh strainer over top. Combine vanilla, water, and espresso powder in small bowl.

2 Whisk egg yolks, sugar, and salt together in separate bowl until combined. Whisk in cream and half-and-half. Transfer mixture to medium saucepan and cook over medium-low heat, stirring constantly and scraping bottom of pot with wooden spoon, until thickened and silky and registers 175 to 180 degrees, 8 to 12 minutes. (Do not let custard overcook or simmer.)

3 Immediately pour custard through fine-mesh strainer over chocolate. Let mixture stand to melt chocolate, about 5 minutes. Add espresso-vanilla mixture and whisk mixture until smooth. Divide mixture evenly among eight 5-ounce ramekins. Gently tap ramekins against counter to settle custard.

4 Let pots de crème cool to room temperature, then cover with plastic wrap and refrigerate until chilled, at least 4 hours or up to 3 days. Before serving, let pots de crème stand at room temperature for 20 to 30 minutes.

5 **For the whipped cream and garnish** Using stand mixer fitted with whisk, whip cream, sugar, and vanilla on medium-low speed until foamy, about 1 minute. Increase speed to high and whip until stiff peaks form, 1 to 3 minutes. Dollop each pot de crème with about 2 tablespoons whipped cream and garnish with cocoa and/or chocolate shavings, if using. Serve.

# banana pudding

serves 12

### pudding

7 slightly underripe large bananas

1½ cups (10½ ounces) sugar

8 large egg yolks

6 tablespoons (1½ ounces) cornstarch

6 cups half-and-half

½ teaspoon salt

3 tablespoons unsalted butter

1 tablespoon vanilla extract

3 tablespoons lemon juice

1 (12-ounce) box vanilla wafers, plus extra for garnish

### whipped topping

1 cup heavy cream, chilled

1 tablespoon sugar

½ teaspoon vanilla extract

1 **For the pudding** Adjust oven rack to upper-middle position and heat oven to 325 degrees. Place 3 unpeeled bananas on baking sheet and bake until skins are completely black, about 20 minutes. Let cool, about 5 minutes, then peel.

2 Meanwhile, whisk ½ cup sugar, egg yolks, and cornstarch in medium bowl until smooth. Bring half-and-half, remaining 1 cup sugar, and salt to simmer in large saucepan over medium heat. Whisk ½ cup simmering half-and-half mixture into egg yolk mixture. Slowly whisk tempered yolk mixture into saucepan. Cook, whisking constantly, until mixture is thick and large bubbles appear on surface, about 2 minutes. Off heat, stir in butter and vanilla.

3 Transfer pudding to food processor, add warm roasted bananas and 2 tablespoons lemon juice, and process until smooth, 30 to 60 seconds. Scrape pudding into large bowl, place lightly greased parchment paper against surface of pudding, and refrigerate until slightly cool, about 45 minutes.

4 Cut remaining bananas into ¼-inch slices and toss in bowl with remaining 1 tablespoon lemon juice. Spoon one-quarter of pudding into 3-quart trifle dish and top with layer of cookies, layer of sliced bananas, and another layer of cookies. Repeat twice more, ending with pudding. Place lightly greased parchment paper against surface of pudding and refrigerate until wafers have softened, at least 8 hours or up to 2 days.

5 **For the whipped topping** Using stand mixer fitted with whisk, whip cream, sugar, and vanilla on medium-low speed until foamy, about 1 minute. Increase speed to high and whip until stiff peaks form, 1 to 3 minutes. Dollop whipped cream over top of banana pudding and arrange extra cookies attractively around edge of dish. Serve.

# new orleans bourbon bread pudding with bourbon sauce

serves 8 to 10

1 (18- to 20-inch) baguette, torn into 1-inch pieces (10 cups)

1 cup golden raisins

¾ cup bourbon

6 tablespoons unsalted butter, cut into 6 pieces and chilled, plus extra for baking dish

8 large egg yolks

1½ cups packed (10½ ounces) light brown sugar

3 cups heavy cream

1 cup whole milk

1 tablespoon vanilla extract

1½ teaspoons ground cinnamon

¼ teaspoon ground nutmeg

¼ teaspoon salt

3 tablespoons granulated sugar

1 recipe Bourbon Sauce (recipe follows)

1  Adjust oven rack to middle position and heat oven to 450 degrees. Arrange bread in single layer on baking sheet and bake until crisp and browned, about 12 minutes, turning pieces over and switching baking sheets halfway through baking. Let bread cool. Reduce oven temperature to 300 degrees.

2  Meanwhile, heat raisins with ½ cup bourbon in small saucepan over medium-high heat until bourbon begins to simmer, 2 to 3 minutes. Strain mixture, reserving bourbon and raisins separately.

3  Butter 13 by 9-inch broiler-safe baking dish. Whisk egg yolks, brown sugar, cream, milk, vanilla, 1 teaspoon cinnamon, nutmeg, and salt together in large bowl. Whisk in reserved bourbon plus remaining ¼ cup bourbon. Add toasted bread and toss until evenly coated. Let mixture sit until bread begins to absorb custard, about 30 minutes, tossing occasionally. If majority of bread is still hard, continue to soak for 15 to 20 minutes.

4  Pour half of bread mixture into prepared baking dish and sprinkle with half of raisins. Pour remaining bread mixture into dish and sprinkle with remaining raisins. Cover with aluminum foil and bake for 45 minutes.

5  Meanwhile, mix granulated sugar and remaining ½ teaspoon cinnamon in small bowl. Using your fingers, cut 6 tablespoons butter into sugar mixture until size of small peas. Remove foil from pudding, sprinkle with butter mixture, and bake, uncovered, until custard is just set, 20 to 25 minutes. Remove pudding from oven and heat broiler.

6  Once broiler is heated, broil pudding until top forms golden crust, about 2 minutes. Transfer to wire rack and let cool for at least 30 minutes or up to 2 hours. Serve.

## bourbon sauce

makes about 1 cup

1½ teaspoons cornstarch

¼ cup bourbon

¾ cup heavy cream

2 tablespoons sugar

Pinch salt

2 teaspoons unsalted butter,
cut into 8 pieces

Whisk cornstarch and 2 tablespoons
bourbon in small bowl until well
combined. Heat cream and sugar in
small saucepan over medium heat
until sugar dissolves. Whisk in
cornstarch mixture and bring to
boil. Reduce heat to low and cook
until sauce thickens, 3 to 5 minutes.
Off heat, stir in salt, butter, and
remaining 2 tablespoons bourbon.
Drizzle warm sauce over individual
servings. (Sauce can be refrigerated
for up to 5 days.)

# tiramisù

serves 10 to 12

2½ cups strong brewed coffee, room temperature

9 tablespoons dark rum

1½ tablespoons instant espresso powder

6 large egg yolks

⅔ cup sugar

¼ teaspoon salt

1½ pounds mascarpone cheese (3 cups)

¾ cup heavy cream, chilled

14 ounces dried ladyfingers (savoiardi)

3½ tablespoons Dutch-processed cocoa

¼ cup grated semisweet or bittersweet chocolate (optional)

> Tiramisù is Ian's all-time favorite dessert and he orders it almost everywhere we go. But the restaurant versions (which I think are all the same brand, sold frozen) don't hold a candle to one that's homemade. This recipe is not only easy, but it makes you look like a rock star. The trick is knowing how long to soak the cookies in the coffee-rum mixture; too long of a soak and the cookies fall apart, but too short of a soak and they stay too crisp. I count the seconds for each cookie as I dip them into the liquid to make sure they are perfect. Make sure to buy dried ladyfingers (sometimes called savoiardi), not fresh ones.
>
> *julia*

1  Stir coffee, 5 tablespoons rum, and espresso in wide bowl or baking dish until espresso dissolves; set aside.

2  Using stand mixer fitted with whisk, whip egg yolks on low speed until just combined. Add sugar and salt and whip on medium-high speed until pale yellow, 1 ½ to 2 minutes, scraping down bowl once or twice. Add remaining ¼ cup rum and whip on medium speed until just combined, 20 to 30 seconds; scrape down bowl. Add mascarpone and whip on medium speed until no lumps remain, 30 to 45 seconds, scraping down bowl once or twice. Transfer mixture to large bowl and set aside.

3  In now-empty mixer bowl, whip cream on medium-low speed until foamy, about 1 minute. Increase speed to high and whip until stiff peaks form, 1 to 3 minutes. Using rubber spatula, fold one-third of whipped cream into mascarpone mixture to lighten, then gently fold in remaining whipped cream until no white streaks remain. Set mascarpone mixture aside.

4  Working with one at a time, drop half of ladyfingers into coffee mixture, roll to coat, remove, and transfer to 13 by 9-inch glass or ceramic baking dish. (Do not submerge ladyfingers in coffee mixture; entire process should take no longer than 2 to 3 seconds for each cookie.) Arrange soaked cookies in single layer in baking dish, breaking or trimming ladyfingers as needed to fit neatly into dish.

5  Spread half of mascarpone mixture over ladyfingers with spatula, spreading mixture to sides and into corners of dish, then smooth surface. Place 2 tablespoons cocoa in fine-mesh strainer and dust cocoa over mascarpone.

6  Repeat dipping and arrangement of ladyfingers; spread remaining mascarpone mixture over ladyfingers and dust with remaining 1 ½ tablespoons cocoa. Wipe edges of dish clean with paper towel. Cover with plastic wrap and refrigerate for at least 6 hours or up to 24 hours. Garnish with grated chocolate, if using; cut into pieces and serve chilled. (Tiramisù can be refrigerated for up to 1 day.)

# coconut layer cake

serves 10 to 12

> Each year, my old elementary school put on a 'cake walk' to raise money for the school. For those that don't know, a cake walk is sort of like musical chairs. You walk around the room with music, and when it stops, you land on a number. A person calls out a number and if it's a match with yours, you get to go pick out a cake made by one of the local ladies. When I was lucky enough to win, I would head straight for one of the statuesque coconut cakes, which always reminded me of a white, fluffy cotillion gown. This recipe is quite possibly my favorite America's Test Kitchen recipe of all time, and I hope that you enjoy it as much as I do, every single year.
>
> *bridget*

### cake

1 large egg plus 5 large whites

¾ cup cream of coconut

¼ cup water

1 teaspoon vanilla extract

1 teaspoon coconut extract

2¼ cups (9 ounces) cake flour

1 cup (7 ounces) sugar

1 tablespoon baking powder

¾ teaspoon salt

12 tablespoons unsalted butter, cut into 12 pieces and softened

2 cups (6 ounces) sweetened shredded coconut

### icing

4 large egg whites

1 cup (7 ounces) sugar

Pinch salt

1 pound (4 sticks) unsalted butter, each stick cut into 6 pieces and softened

¼ cup cream of coconut

1 teaspoon coconut extract

1 teaspoon vanilla extract

**1  For the cake**  Adjust oven rack to lower-middle position and heat oven to 325 degrees. Grease two 9-inch round cake pans, line with parchment paper, grease parchment, and flour pans. Whisk egg and whites together in large liquid measuring cup. Whisk in cream of coconut, water, vanilla, and coconut extract.

**2**  Mix flour, sugar, baking powder, and salt in bowl of stand mixer. Using paddle on low speed, beat in butter, 1 piece at a time, until only pea-size pieces remain, about 1 minute. Add half of egg mixture, increase speed to medium-high, and beat until light and fluffy, about 1 minute. Reduce speed to medium-low, add remaining egg mixture, and beat until incorporated, about 30 seconds. Give batter final stir by hand.

**3**  Divide batter evenly between prepared pans, smooth tops, and gently tap pans on counter to settle batter. Bake cakes until toothpick inserted in centers comes out clean, about 30 minutes, rotating pans halfway through baking.

**4**  Let cakes cool in pans for 10 minutes. Remove cakes from pans, discard parchment, and let cool completely on wire rack, about 2 hours. (Cakes can be stored at room temperature for up to 1 day or frozen for up to 1 month; defrost cakes at room temperature.) Meanwhile, spread shredded coconut on rimmed baking sheet and toast in oven until shreds are mix of golden brown and white, 15 to 20 minutes, stirring 2 or 3 times; let cool.

**5  For the icing**  Combine egg whites, sugar, and salt in bowl of stand mixer and set over medium saucepan filled with 1 inch of barely simmering water (do not let bottom of bowl touch water). Cook, whisking constantly, until mixture is opaque and registers 120 degrees, about 2 minutes.

**6** Remove bowl from heat. Using whisk on high speed, whip egg white mixture until glossy, sticky, and barely warm (80 degrees), about 7 minutes. Reduce speed to medium-high and whip in butter, 1 piece at a time, followed by cream of coconut, coconut extract, and vanilla, scraping down bowl as needed. Continue to whip at medium-high speed until combined, about 1 minute.

**7** Using long serrated knife, cut 1 horizontal line around sides of each layer; then, following scored lines, cut each layer into 2 even layers.

**8** Line edges of cake platter with 4 strips of parchment paper to keep platter clean, and place small dab of frosting in center of platter to anchor cake. Place 1 cake layer on platter. Spread ¾ cup frosting evenly over top, right to edge of cake. Top with second cake layer and press lightly to adhere. Repeat with more frosting and remaining cake layers. Spread remaining frosting evenly over top and sides of cake. To smooth frosting, run edge of offset spatula around cake sides and over top. Sprinkle top of cake evenly with toasted coconut, then press remaining toasted coconut into sides of cake. Carefully remove parchment strips before serving. (Frosted cake can be refrigerated for up to 1 day; bring to room temperature before serving.)

# goat cheese and lemon cheesecake with hazelnut crust

serves 12 to 14

*Cooking at Home with Bridget and Julia*

> "I grew up eating my oma's cheesecake, which used cottage cheese instead of cream cheese for the filling and crushed-up zwieback crackers instead of graham crackers for the crust. For me, this version set the bar for what cheesecake should be and no other recipe came close until this unique goat cheese and lemon cheesecake came along. I love the tanginess that the goat cheese adds, and the easy lemon curd complements the cheesecake perfectly, adding a bright burst of lemony flavor. Plus, the hazelnut flavor in the crust is pure genius. The biggest trick to this recipe is wrapping the springform pan tightly with a double layer of heavy-duty aluminum foil to prevent any water from the water bath from sogging out the crust during baking."
>
> *julia*

### hazelnut crust

⅓ cup hazelnuts, toasted and skinned

3 tablespoons sugar

3 ounces Nabisco Barnum's Animals Crackers or Social Tea Biscuits

3 tablespoons unsalted butter, melted and cooled

### cheesecake

1¼ cups (8¾ ounces) sugar

1 tablespoon grated lemon zest plus ¼ cup juice (2 lemons)

1 pound cream cheese, cut into 1-inch pieces and softened

8 ounces goat cheese, cut into 1-inch pieces and softened

4 large eggs, room temperature

2 teaspoons vanilla extract

¼ teaspoon salt

½ cup heavy cream

### lemon curd

⅓ cup lemon juice (2 lemons)

2 large eggs plus 1 large yolk

½ cup (3½ ounces) sugar

2 tablespoons unsalted butter, cut into ½-inch cubes and chilled

1 tablespoon heavy cream

¼ teaspoon vanilla extract

Pinch salt

**1  For the hazelnut crust**  Adjust oven rack to lower-middle position and heat oven to 325 degrees. Process hazelnuts and sugar in food processor until finely ground, about 30 seconds. Add crackers and process until finely ground, about 30 seconds. While pulsing processor, add butter in slow, steady stream until mixture is evenly moistened and resembles wet sand, about 10 pulses.

2  Sprinkle mixture into 9-inch springform pan and press firmly into compact layer with bottom of dry measuring cup. Bake until fragrant and beginning to brown, 10 to 15 minutes. Let crust cool for 30 minutes, then wrap outside of pan with 2 pieces heavy-duty foil and set inside roasting pan.

**3  For the cheesecake**  Process ¼ cup sugar and lemon zest in food processor until sugar is very yellow, about 15 seconds; combine with remaining 1 cup sugar.

4  Using stand mixer fitted with paddle, beat cream cheese and goat cheese on low speed for 5 seconds. With mixer running, add sugar mixture in steady stream. Increase speed to medium and beat until smooth, about 3 minutes. Reduce speed to medium-low and add eggs, 2 at a time, until incorporated, scraping down bowl after each addition. Add lemon juice, vanilla, and salt and beat for 5 seconds. Add cream and beat for 5 seconds.

5  Pour batter into prepared springform pan. Fill roasting pan with enough hot tap water to come

halfway up sides of pan. Bake until center jiggles slightly and registers 150 degrees, 55 to 60 minutes.

**6** Turn off oven, prop open oven door with wooden spoon, and let cake sit in water bath for 1 hour longer. Transfer springform pan, without foil, to wire rack and let cool to room temperature, running paring knife around edge of cake every hour. Wrap tightly in plastic wrap and refrigerate until cold, about 3 hours.

**7 For the lemon curd** While cheesecake bakes, heat lemon juice in small saucepan over medium heat until hot but not boiling. Whisk eggs and yolk in medium bowl, then gradually whisk in sugar. Whisking constantly, slowly pour hot lemon juice into egg mixture. Return mixture to saucepan and cook, stirring constantly, until mixture is thick and registers 170 degrees, about 3 minutes. Immediately remove from heat and stir in butter, followed by cream, vanilla, and salt. Strain through fine-mesh strainer into bowl. Cover surface of curd directly with plastic wrap and refrigerate until needed.

**8** When cheesecake is cold, spread lemon curd evenly over top while still in pan. Cover tightly with plastic wrap and refrigerate until set, about 4 hours. (Lemon cheesecake can be refrigerated, covered, for up to 1 day.) To serve, remove sides of springform pan and cut cake into wedges.

# florentine lace cookies

makes 24 cookies

2 cups slivered almonds

¾ cup heavy cream

½ cup (3½ ounces) sugar

4 tablespoons unsalted butter, cut into 4 pieces

¼ cup orange marmalade

3 tablespoons all-purpose flour

1 teaspoon vanilla extract

¼ teaspoon grated orange zest

¼ teaspoon salt

4 ounces bittersweet chocolate, chopped fine

"

I've loved these flat, crisp almond-citrus-chocolate cookies ever since I was a kid. Yet I never made these fussy little cookies myself until this recipe came out of the test kitchen because most recipes are complicated and unpredictable. Other recipes involve tempering the hot sugar mixture that becomes the base of the dough, but the ATK version simply removes it from the heat when it thickens and begins to brown. Note that these cookies are baked much darker than most cookies. "

*julia*

1  Adjust oven racks to upper-middle and lower-middle positions and heat oven to 350 degrees. Line 2 baking sheets with parchment paper. Process almonds in food processor until they resemble coarse sand, about 30 seconds.

2  Bring cream, sugar, and butter to boil in medium saucepan over medium-high heat. Cook, stirring frequently, until mixture begins to thicken, 5 to 6 minutes. Continue to cook, stirring constantly, until mixture begins to brown at edges and is thick enough to leave trail that doesn't immediately fill in when spatula is scraped along pan bottom, 1 to 2 minutes longer (it's OK if some darker speckles appear in mixture). Remove pan from heat and stir in almonds, marmalade, flour, vanilla, orange zest, and salt until combined.

3  Drop 6 level tablespoons of dough at least 3½ inches apart on each prepared sheet. When cool enough to handle, use your damp fingers to press each portion into 2½-inch circle.

4  Bake until deep brown from edge to edge, 15 to 17 minutes, switching and rotating sheets halfway through baking. Transfer cookies, still on parchment, to wire racks and let cool. Let baking sheets cool for 10 minutes, line with fresh parchment, and repeat portioning and baking remaining dough.

5  Microwave 3 ounces chocolate in bowl at 50 percent power, stirring frequently, until about two-thirds melted, 1 to 2 minutes. Remove bowl from microwave, add remaining 1 ounce chocolate, and stir until melted, returning to microwave for no more than 5 seconds at a time to complete melting if necessary. Transfer chocolate to small zipper-lock bag and snip off corner, making hole no larger than $1/16$ inch.

6  Transfer cooled cookies directly to wire racks. Pipe zigzag of chocolate over each cookie, distributing chocolate evenly among all cookies. Refrigerate until chocolate is set, about 30 minutes, before serving. (Cookies can be stored at cool room temperature for up to 4 days.)

# conversions and equivalents

Some say cooking is a science and an art. We would say that geography has a hand in it, too. Flours and sugars manufactured in the United Kingdom and elsewhere will feel and taste different from those manufactured in the United States. So we cannot promise that the loaf of bread you bake in Canada or England will taste the same as a loaf baked in the States, but we can offer guidelines for converting weights and measures. We also recommend that you rely on your instincts when making our recipes. Refer to the visual cues provided. If the dough hasn't "come together, in a ball" as described, you may need to add more flour—even if the recipe doesn't tell you to. You be the judge.

The recipes in this book were developed using standard U.S. measures following U.S. government guidelines. The charts below offer equivalents for U.S. and metric measures. All conversions are approximate and have been rounded up or down to the nearest whole number.

*example*

1 teaspoon = 4.9292 milliliters,
        rounded up to 5 milliliters

1 ounce = 28.3495 grams,
        rounded down to 28 grams

## volume conversions

| U.S. | METRIC |
| --- | --- |
| 1 teaspoon | 5 milliliters |
| 2 teaspoons | 10 milliliters |
| 1 tablespoon | 15 milliliters |
| 2 tablespoons | 30 milliliters |
| ¼ cup | 59 milliliters |
| ⅓ cup | 79 milliliters |
| ½ cup | 118 milliliters |
| ¾ cup | 177 milliliters |
| 1 cup | 237 milliliters |
| 1¼ cups | 296 milliliters |
| 1½ cups | 355 milliliters |
| 2 cups (1 pint) | 473 milliliters |
| 2½ cups | 591 milliliters |
| 3 cups | 710 milliliters |
| 4 cups (1 quart) | 0.946 liter |
| 1.06 quarts | 1 liter |
| 4 quarts (1 gallon) | 3.8 liters |

## weight conversions

| OUNCES | GRAMS |
| --- | --- |
| ½ | 14 |
| ¾ | 21 |
| 1 | 28 |
| 1½ | 43 |
| 2 | 57 |
| 2½ | 71 |
| 3 | 85 |
| 3½ | 99 |
| 4 | 113 |
| 4½ | 128 |
| 5 | 142 |
| 6 | 170 |
| 7 | 198 |
| 8 | 227 |
| 9 | 255 |
| 10 | 283 |
| 12 | 340 |
| 16 (1 pound) | 454 |

## conversion for common baking ingredients

Baking is an exacting science. Because measuring by weight is far more accurate than measuring by volume, and thus more likely to produce reliable results, in our recipes we provide ounce measures in addition to cup measures for many ingredients. Refer to the chart below to convert these measures into grams.

| INGREDIENT | OUNCES | GRAMS |
| --- | --- | --- |
| **Flour** | | |
| 1 cup all-purpose flour* | 5 | 142 |
| 1 cup cake flour | 4 | 113 |
| 1 cup whole-wheat flour | 5½ | 156 |
| **Sugar** | | |
| 1 cup granulated (white) sugar | 7 | 198 |
| 1 cup packed brown sugar (light or dark) | 7 | 198 |
| 1 cup confectioners' sugar | 4 | 113 |
| **Cocoa Powder** | | |
| 1 cup cocoa powder | 3 | 85 |
| **Butter†** | | |
| 4 tablespoons (½ stick, or ¼ cup) | 2 | 57 |
| 8 tablespoons (1 stick, or ½ cup) | 4 | 113 |
| 16 tablespoons (2 sticks, or 1 cup) | 8 | 227 |

\* U.S. all-purpose flour, the most frequently used flour in this book, does not contain leaveners, as some European flours do. These leavened flours are called self-rising or self-raising. If you are using self-rising flour, take this into consideration before adding leavening to a recipe.

† In the United States, butter is sold both salted and unsalted. We generally recommend unsalted butter. If you are using salted butter, take this into consideration before adding salt to a recipe.

## oven temperatures

| FAHRENHEIT | CELSIUS | GAS MARK |
| --- | --- | --- |
| 225 | 105 | ¼ |
| 250 | 120 | ½ |
| 275 | 135 | 1 |
| 300 | 150 | 2 |
| 325 | 165 | 3 |
| 350 | 180 | 4 |
| 375 | 190 | 5 |
| 400 | 200 | 6 |
| 425 | 220 | 7 |
| 450 | 230 | 8 |
| 475 | 245 | 9 |

## converting temperatures from an instant-read thermometer

We include doneness temperatures in many of the recipes in this book. We recommend an instant-read thermometer for the job. Refer to the above table to convert Fahrenheit degrees to Celsius. Or, for temperatures not represented in the chart, use this simple formula:

Subtract 32 degrees from the Fahrenheit reading, then divide the result by 1.8 to find the Celsius reading.

*example*
"Roast chicken until thighs register 175 degrees."

to convert
175°F – 32 = 143°
143° ÷ 1.8 = 79.44°C, rounded down to 79°C

# index